Forgiveness
equals FORTUNE

Liah Holtzman
and
Lauren O. Thyme

FORGIVENESS EQUALS FORTUNE

Liah Holtzman
www.LiahHoltzman.com
liah_h@hotmail.com

....

Cover illustration by Fedhar
Original cover design and book illustrations by Shayla Roberts
Second edition cover design by Stephanie Lucas

Volcano and Bridge illustrations by Devon Q. Thyme.
Concept for illustrations on pages 49 – 50 designed by Stephanie Lucas
Illustrations on pages 49 – 50 drawn by Nicole Jordan
Background Texture on Cover "Designed by Freepik"

FORGIVENESS EQUALS FORTUNE

I f someone told you they had a clear-cut instruction book about forgiving, with an easy step-by-step method, which produced immediate fortunate results, would you be interested in reading it? *"Forgiveness equals Fortune" is that book.*

After decades of research, experimentation, demonstrations, seminars and consultations, I have **total certainty** that this book and its forgiveness method produce positive results. Please allow my certainty and experience to assist you to generate miracles in your life through the effective use of forgiveness. The *Forgiveness equals Fortune* book is not simply about gaining **new** information. The book's main focus is on **doing** the forgiveness work and is designed to **encourage** you to take action, using simple and effective methods.

Is an area of your life not working as well as you would like? Then, consider whom you might forgive in order to remove blockages to the flow of goodness into that area.

If you have difficulty naturally letting go of deep hurts, grudges and grievances, please follow the *Forgiveness equals Fortune* steps to kick start your forgiveness engine. You may mentally do the exercises, write them, say them out loud or practice with a friend or a forgiveness coach. All methods are beneficial.

Doing forgiveness with a partner is probably the *most effective*. If you run into difficulty, you may want to work with someone knowledgeable or trained, who can assist you to move through blocks and resistances which are hindering positive results.

Once you understand the basic principles of the method through practice, the art of forgiving will become a natural foundation upon which to live and enjoy your life. From my heart to yours, I encourage you to build your forgiveness muscles – developing and maintaining your forgiveness strength will be well worth your time and effort.

FORGIVENESS EQUALS FORTUNE

TABLE OF CONTENTS

TABLE OF CONTENTS

ACKNOWLEDGEMENTS

I acknowledge and thank my friend, Lauren O. Thyme, for making the dream of this forgiveness book come true and for being the driving force behind the first and second edition. I'm so grateful she knew what to do.

I also thank Claudia Dorda for recognizing who I am and the importance of forgiveness, then taking action to make the Spanish edition of this book possible - as well as inviting me to Argentina.

Many thanks to Patricia Consoli for doing a superb job on the original Spanish translation.

I am also grateful to Michael Brownlee and Marie Hanthorn for supporting me to self-publish this book, my Forgiver-ism booklet and my *Forgiveness equals Fortune* CD. Their friendship and expertise empowered me.

Also, I wish to thank Stephanie Lucas (lovingly called Steph) for her skill and patience in updating the *Forgiveness equals Fortune* book into current technology, redesigning the cover, formatting the book and lovingly guiding me through the complexities and emotional ups and downs of rewriting and publishing a life-changing book on forgiveness.

I am so grateful to Nicole Jordan for drawing the faces for the Alternative Perceptions of Reality section. Nicole is a talented face painter and successfully taught herself to draw this type of illustration specifically for this book. Each face conveys a lot of character and emotion with just a few lines. Nice job Nicole.

Thanks to Dennis Deppey for the cute name, "Pity Party Patty."

My sincere acknowledgement, praise and thanks to Rev. Michele Whittington at Creative Living Fellowship, a Church of Religious Science in Phoenix, Arizona, for being the Minister of my Spiritual Home. Our tag line is "A Community of Care Opening Hearts and Incubating Dreams." My participation at CLF has gently opened my heart, cleared my mind and is incubating amazing dreams I didn't even know I had.

I acknowledge myself for completing this forgiveness book and constantly being willing to look at the areas of my life where forgiveness is still needed - no matter how challenging that might be. Thank goodness for my connection to Infinite Intelligence.

ACKNOWLEDGEMENTS

CHAPTER 1

WHO ME? UNFORGIVING?

In 1976, I had absolutely no idea I was unforgiving until someone told me that certain aspects of my personality would make me very critical. I'll always remember her saying: "Liah, you will be one of the least forgiving people in the world."

Well, I never *forgave her for saying that!*

This interaction was an eye-opener for me. I began to understand myself so much more. I decided to enroll in self-improvement and self-awareness seminars. All were extremely valuable, although afterwards I started experiencing confusion and turmoil. I felt like I was surfing in an emotional cesspool.

In November 1977, I saw a flyer about *Rebirthing*. I didn't know what rebirthing was, but I intuitively knew it was correct for me.

Leonard Orr developed the process of Rebirthing. His seminar on Rebirthing prepared me for the fastest self-awareness method I'd learned up to that time. Rebirthing is a breathing technique that restores the breath and heals the negative effects from birth trauma.

After realizing the negative influence my own birth was having in my daily life, I totally threw myself into the process. I studied with Leonard in Houston for a year. Then I moved to San Francisco to be his personal assistant and to manage his newsletter called *The Money Loveletter*. This newsletter had been in existence for several years, was fairly successful and had produced a certain amount of steady income. However, when I took over the management of the *Loveletter*, the income suddenly DROPPED. I was not very happy about this.

Leonard taught me *thought is creative*, which means I am totally responsible for everything that happens in and around my life. Therefore, in some way, I was creating this decrease in income for the newsletter. The concept that reality is our own creation is so important I've devoted a whole chapter to it.

By reliving my birth through Rebirthing, I realized my present-day situations were re-creations of the past. In addition, I read *Dynamic Laws of Prosperity* by Catherine Ponder, who stated that the lack of forgiveness blocks prosperity.

CHAPTER 1
WHO ME? UNFORGIVING?

The words "Liah, you will be one of the least forgiving people in the world," rang in my ears. Who and what was I not forgiving?

I realized I was upset with Leonard. He had personality traits similar to one of my past loving partners, whom I had not forgiven.

I looked deeper still. My father had those same traits - and I had never forgiven him. Could these be the blocks to my prosperity?

Since I was interested in increasing my income, I decided to do an experiment. At the time, I had a long list of unresolved issues with my father. With my grievance list in hand, I started forgiving him. As I did, I was astonished as waves of emotion poured out of me. I spent nine hours that day forgiving my father.

Thirty minutes after I finished forgiving my father, I went downstairs to the lobby of the Rebirthing Center where I lived. Just as I arrived, two people walked in the front door. I approached them and introduced myself.

"Oh, you're Liah! I'm Joe, and this is Judy from Washington. We dropped by to give you a tithe for the *Money Loveletter*," and he handed me $230. I had spent nine hours forgiving my father, which then unblocked the flow of money to me and the *Money Loveletter*. Catherine Ponder was right. Forgiveness works.

I was so excited that I ran back upstairs and started forgiving *everybody* in my life!

The more I forgave, the more money came in. That year I doubled my income as I had another great business opportunity appear.

In addition to the *Money Loveletter*, I organized the *Loving Relationships Training* created by Sondra Ray, a self-awareness training about relationships which also incorporates Rebirthing. As part of my duties with the LRT, I was to create Graduate Evenings that were informational and supportive.

At one point, I decided to conduct a Forgiveness Evening for the graduates. Although I didn't consider myself an expert in forgiveness, I had created results in my own life by forgiving. I had heard the expression, "teaching is learning twice," and I wanted to learn more. I put together some forgiveness information with a forgiveness process and presented it to a group of twenty people.

As we did the forgiveness process, I was shocked because many people began sobbing. I thought I was the only one who responded so intensely. Forgiveness had a profound effect on everyone in the room. That's when I decided to expand and perfect a forgiveness seminar.

In 1981, I presented my first *Forgiveness equals Fortune* seminar in San Francisco. Since I was still experimenting with the principle of forgiveness, I followed up later with the graduates of my seminar. They were producing results too. Some people produced money results, which I call *Fortunes of the Pocketbook*. Others produced new clients, new lovers, new and better jobs, physical healing and began attaining their goals and dreams. These types of results I call *Fortunes of the Heart*.

Obviously, people were producing very positive results in their lives immediately after the seminar. I noticed most results seemed to occur during the first nine days.

I have presented hundreds of *Forgiveness equals Fortune* seminars since that time. What started out as my personal lesson in forgiveness became my gift to the world.

John Randolph Price, in *The Planetary Commission*, states this principle clearly:

> "*Under the law of compensation, for every lesson to be learned in a lifetime, there is also a gift to share with others - a talent for you to utilize in helping other souls master their challenges, learn their lessons and awaken to the truth.*"

At some point during the first six years of researching and experimenting with forgiveness principles, I realized I had a book inside of me. I laboriously wrote a number of rough drafts. However, writing didn't come easily to me and I put the project aside. I felt even more pressure when an astrologer advised me the stars were demanding I write and publish a book. Although I felt somewhat guilty, I realized the book would be written in its own time.

Speaking of time, Lauren O. Thyme and I met when she took my *Forgiveness equals Fortune* seminar in Sacramento. She also saw me at the Loving Relationships Training in the Bay area, but we didn't connect personally either time.

After we both moved to Orange County, California, a mutual friend, Ellen Tews, spoke about us to each other.

When Lauren saw me, she said to Ellen, "Oh - Liah Holtzman! I know her from up north. She is the person who does the forgiveness seminar. What a small world."

Later Lauren took the *Forgiveness equals Fortune* seminar a second time - which our friend Ellen produced at her home. Lauren received even more value from the second seminar and was inspired to write a couple of fairy tales from the ideas and principles presented. The fairy tale, "The Rose and the Gladiola," which is included in this book, became part of her first book, Thymely Tales.

One evening in December of 1986, Lauren came up to me at a baby shower and divulged, "You may think this is egotistical, but I got a message that we are supposed to write a book on forgiveness. I believe in the value of your work and I want to help get the book out of you and onto paper to share it with the Universe."

I literally jumped up and down with glee. I said, "Are you kidding me? I know I'm supposed to write a book, but I didn't have the slightest idea how I was going to do it. You are an answer to my prayers."

Good "timing" ~~

Throughout the months of writing together, Lauren and I sometimes experienced great release and joy. Other days we ran into our own negativity and pain. Sometimes just absorbing the words we wrote would create reactions in us that promoted more personal clearing, awareness and forgiveness. We became friends, and our individual lives and relationships were deeply affected by this collaboration.

Our partnership developed into a whole new level of experience for us. At times during our financial negotiations, we became dismally fearful and stuck for a week, until we finally reached a win/win solution. Regardless of the obstacles, we continued writing, always knowing that the book was a divine project of love and practicing the forgiveness principles ourselves. More than merely a writing project, the creation of this book has been a growth experience for both of us.

I acknowledge Lauren for her inspiration, her contribution, her wisdom and her love for both me and the principles of forgiveness. Her contribution may be invisible at times, yet permeates the book, as she fully supported me to accomplish this enormous task.

Both Lauren and I are planetary servers and believe forgiveness is one of the most powerful and effective tools to heal our planet. Forgiveness has had a vast impact on our own healing process, and we share that with you.

Since forgiveness is so powerful, you too may experience obstacles to reading this book. So please keep the following metaphor in mind while reading.

GROCERY STORE METAPHOR

When you go into a grocery store, you walk up and down the aisles and buy what you want or need. You don't stop shopping if there's something on the shelves you don't like or want to buy - like prunes, liver, alfalfa sprouts, sugar or tofu.

The *Forgiveness equals Fortune* Workbook is my grocery store. On the shelves there may be ideas, concepts and philosophies you don't believe, like or want. I don't ask you to "buy" everything I say, merely that you suspend judgment and remain open. Sometimes a concept will stimulate an unpleasant memory of parents, teachers, preachers, or annoying individuals. If this happens, you may shut down, get angry or even want to stop reading.

However, if you remain open to these ideas, they will become more appealing the more you digest them. Some ideas and concepts are an acquired taste. Others can be left behind on the shelf when you're done shopping.

On the other hand, as I rewrite this book decades later, you may find some of the ideas have been around for years and are in alignment with your current thinking.

In any event, please open your mind and your heart while working with the *Forgiveness equals Fortune* theory. Be gentle and kind to yourself while reading. Stay focused and breathe yourself through to the end. Your rewards could be great!

CHAPTER 1
WHO ME? UNFORGIVING?

CHAPTER 2
WHAT IS FORGIVENESS?

Forgiveness is a vitally important principle in all world religions and spiritual thought. Yet many people are fuzzy about the meaning of forgiveness, don't know how to experience it or how to do it.

Forgiveness is a simple, yet commonly misunderstood word, so let's first define it. Webster's Dictionary defines forgiveness as:

- to cease to feel resentment against;
- to grant remission of an offense, debt, fine or penalty;
- to pardon;
- to free from the consequences of an injurious act or crime;
- to grant pardon to an offender;
- inclined to overlook offenses;
- compassionate.

A Course in Miracles says:

- Forgiveness is still and quietly does nothing. It merely looks and waits and judges not.
- Forgiveness is the key to happiness.
- Forgiveness sweeps away distortions and opens the hidden altar to the truth.
- Forgiveness is the means by which the world is healed.

Other interesting definitions of forgiveness are:

- To give up resentment against or the desire to punish;
- To stop being angry with;
- To give up your justifiable right to revenge;
- To give up that which you are holding onto;
- To let go of negative energy and divorce the past;
- To lift the blockages within us to the flow of life;
- To gain a sense of peace and harmony again;

- To take total responsibility for everything in your life;
- To produce the reunion of souls;
- To live free in the present moment.

Forgiveness is like bankruptcy. All debts are forgiven and you start over with a clean slate.

The most memorable definition, and the inspiration for the cover illustration of this book, comes from Mark Twain:

> *"Forgiveness is the fragrance the violet sheds on the heel that just crushed it."*

WHAT FORGIVENESS IS NOT

Dr. Sidney B. Simon and Suzanne Simon, in their book, Forgiveness: *How to Make Peace with Your Past and Get on with Your Life*, give some examples of what forgiveness *isn't*. Below is a synopsis of some of that information:

Forgiveness is not done for someone else. Forgiveness is an act of self-care. You forgive to stop hurting yourself and make your life work better. When you have anger or other negative emotions towards someone, you suffer the consequences of your feelings.

Forgiveness is not condoning. The act of forgiving does not imply right or wrong. Judgment is not involved in forgiveness and neither is an apology. You merely take responsibility for the situation and release any suppressed negative emotions.

Forgiveness is not forgetting. The mind does not forget anything. Scientists have discovered the mind stores everything we experience, taste, feel, see or hear, whether we are awake or asleep, conscious or unconscious. The mind acts like a computer with unlimited storage capacity. Sometimes people do not recall events, but the effects of those events are still operating within the psyche. Forgiving is not forgetting, but remembering and letting go.

You may find, after forgiving, the memory will fade. That is what is meant by forgive and forget.

Forgiveness is not absolution. Forgiving does not vindicate any hurtful act. One is still held accountable for one's actions. A criminal action must be treated under due process of law.

INNOCENT OR GUILTY?

Forgiveness means we let go of our judgments and negative feelings toward another person. Although we forgive criminals, society may still punish them. To keep order, society's laws must be upheld. We forgive criminals - and put them in jail. Criminals certainly may forgive themselves, even though they broke the law.

Survivors and victims are encouraged to practice forgiveness toward perpetrators in order to clear and heal themselves.

FORGIVENESS HEALS - HATRED HARMS

Oprah Winfrey aired a show many years ago about unforgiving victims and their current situations.

One woman, shot by a gang of men, decided she could never forgive them. The doctors were unable to remove the bullet, which she still painfully carries in her stomach. She is an angry, bitter, unhappy person.

The *Courage to Heal*, a book for adult survivors of child sexual abuse, tells a similar story. A woman had been abused as a young child by her father and refused to forgive him. She delighted in thinking angry, vengeful thoughts about him, even going to the cemetery and dancing on his grave. Shortly thereafter, she contracted cancer and for two years suffered agonizing pain with her illness.

I wonder what would happen if these two women released their anger through forgiveness?

HOW CAN YOU TELL YOU NEED TO FORGIVE? - EXERCISE

You may say you don't need to forgive, that there is no one in your life to forgive. However, this belief may not be accurate and here is a way to test your belief:

Close your eyes and relax. Now, think of someone you resent or dislike - someone who has hurt you.

Notice how you feel. Notice your jaw, your heart, your stomach and your breathing. Notice your overall feeling while thinking of that person.

Do you notice: your jaw tightens, breathing becomes labored, a headache appears, your chest hurts, and/or palms get clammy? In other words, suddenly you don't feel as good.

Now take three deep breaths and release your thoughts of that person.

This exercise lasted approximately two minutes. Imagine what is happening in your body if you resent or feel hurt by one or more persons for many years? All of those feelings build up and can produce stress and pain.

Now - think of someone you love, someone you are clear with. If you can't think of someone, think of some thing that you love, like a flower, the ocean or an animal.

Once again notice how you feel. Be aware of your jaw, your heart, your stomach and your breathing. Pay attention to your overall feeling while thinking of the person or thing you love.

Do you notice a sense of peace and relaxation, a smile touching your lips, easy breathing, an open and light heart and chest? In other words, do you feel good?

MISCONCEPTIONS ABOUT FORGIVENESS

Forgiveness has been misunderstood and therefore misused in the past. These thoughts may help clear up some of the forgiveness confusion.

Forgiveness is not reconciliation - although it may set the stage for it. You don't have to spend time with the person you forgive or become "bosom buddies" just because you forgave someone. You don't have to invite them over for dinner. In fact, you don't ever have to see them again. Whew - aren't you glad?

You don't have to inform the person that you have forgiven them. Since forgiveness is an internal process you do for yourself, there is no one to notify. In fact, if you tell someone you are forgiving them, this can be a sneaky way of letting them know you were unhappy with them. To report to a person you are forgiving them encourages confrontation and puts the "forgiven" on the defensive.

Forgiveness has no conditions attached to it. Forgiveness is unconditional. Conditions commonly attached to forgiveness are:

- I will forgive you *if* you do something for me.

- *When* you forgive me, I'll forgive you.

- I will forgive you only *if* you change.

- I'll forgive you *if* you say you're sorry.

- I'll forgive you *if* you never do it again.

Forgiveness doesn't make you or the other person more spiritual. If you are using forgiveness to become more spiritual, holy or devout, you've missed the point. Forgiveness is a paradox. Forgiveness is spiritual, but it will not make you spiritual. Forgiveness does not prove you are better than someone else. Forgiveness sees perfection in all things and all people. Forgiveness doesn't imply the other person is more spiritual either, nor more worthy or better than you. Forgive the other person in order to feel more joyous.

WE SEE ONLY IN FRAGMENTS, NOT THE TOTAL PICTURE

Our erroneous and incomplete judgments are one important reason why we must forgive. Blaming and judging comes from a limited point of view.

The following story poignantly depicts two important elements of forgiveness:

1. We cannot see the whole picture; and

2. Since we cannot see the totality, our judgments and perceptions might be inaccurate.

THE HORSE STORY

There was a poor, old man who lived in a small village. He owned a beautiful white horse. Kings offered fabulous prices for the horse, but the man would say: "This horse is my friend." The man was poor, but he never sold the horse.

One morning he found the horse was gone from the stable. The whole village gathered and said, "You foolish old man. We knew someday the horse would be stolen. You should have sold it. What a misfortune!"

The old man replied, "That is not necessarily true. The horse is simply not in the stable. This is the fact. Everything else is a judgment. Who knows if it is a misfortune or a blessing?"

People laughed at the old man. They knew he was a little crazy. But after fifteen days, the horse suddenly returned. He had not been stolen but had gone visiting. Not only that, a dozen wild horses returned with him.

Again, the people gathered and said, "Old man, you were right. The disappearance of your horse is not a misfortune. It has indeed proved to be a blessing."

The old man said, "Again you are going too far. Just say the horse came back. Who knows whether its return is a blessing or not? When you read a single word, how can you judge the whole book?"

The people did not say much, but they knew he was wrong. After all, twelve beautiful horses had come.

The old man's only son started to train the wild horses. But a week later he fell from a horse and broke his legs. The people gathered and again they judged. "You were right. Getting twelve horses was a misfortune. Your son, who is your only support, has lost the use of his legs. Now you are poorer than ever."

The old man said, "You are obsessed with judgment. Only say my son has broken his legs. Nobody knows whether this is a misfortune or a blessing. Life comes in fragments and more is never revealed."

After a few weeks, the country went to war. All the young men in town were forced into the military. Only the old man's son was left, because he was crippled. The whole town cried because they knew most of the young men would never return. They said to the old man, "You were right. This is a blessing. Your son may be crippled, but he is still with you. Our sons are gone forever."

The old man said again, "Nobody knows. Say only this: Your sons have entered the army and my son has not. We cannot know whether it is a blessing or a misfortune. Stop judging or you will always be obsessed with fragments and live in faulty conclusions."

(A story from a **Neo-Tarot** deck by Bhagwan Shree Rajneesh, also known as Osho.)

CHAPTER 2
WHAT IS FORGIVENESS?

CHAPTER 3
RECEIVING FORTUNE

As I operated the *Money Loveletter* and practiced forgiveness, it became obvious that forgiveness sets wonderful things in motion. After forgiving, other people and I experienced miracles, synchronicity and fortunate changes. What is **fortune** and what do I mean by fortune?

There are different aspects of fortune. During the Forgiveness equals Fortune seminar, the participants make a list of fortunes they want to receive. Some of the fortunate results participants received after taking my seminar are listed under the appropriate definitions.

According to Webster, fortune means:

◆ *Possessions, especially money and property*...

Peter went home after the Forgiveness equals Fortune seminar and received a call that his weekly income would be doubled in nine days.

Al forgave his mom. Shortly thereafter she unexpectedly sent him a check for $600.

Bill barely scraped together the money to take the seminar. He forgave a family member. Five days later he received a $650 check from another family member.

◆ *Attributes and inherent qualities...*

A woman attended the Forgiveness seminar. She can now communicate better with her ex-husband which is important to her since they are still raising two children.

Felice was inspired to fast and lost weight.

June forgave herself. The next day she felt happier than ever before. For the first time, she felt a sense of satisfaction about herself.

- ***The turns and courses of luck accompanying the progress of an individual; a hypothetical force or power that determines events and issues for persons or causes...***

  Steve, a contractor, got a new contract the day after taking the seminar.

  Fran participated in her first seminar and found a new apartment. After taking her second seminar, a new lover came into her life, after a seven-year dry spell.

  Albert took the seminar and got three new clients the next day.

- ***Condition in life as determined by material possessions; large possessions; riches or wealth...***

  Gayle decreased her debts by $700 in seven days.

  Someone gave Laurie a stereo to use for awhile, which brought her great pleasure with no financial expenditure.

  Linda was able to buy herself an expensive gift now without worrying about finances, as she did before.

Webster defines fortune as being associated with luck. Yet I believe we are the designers of our destiny, and there is no such thing as coincidence or luck. Therefore, everything I am or have is a direct result of my thoughts, words and consciousness. To me fortune includes:

- ***Physical, mental, emotional, and spiritual well-being...***

  During the seminar, after the Physical Release Visualization, a man came running up to me, wiggling his neck and shoulders. He said "Look! I can move the top three vertebrae of my spine. They have been locked in place for years." A couple of years later I saw him at a wedding. He said his back had been permanently healed.

One person did the *Forgiveness equals Fortune* seminar, released her bitterness and noticed her voice changed for the better.

A woman who was molested as a young girl had developed a vaginal infection no doctor could heal. She forgave the man who sexually abused her. Three days later her infection disappeared.

One lady desired a new lover. That night she left the seminar with a new lover. Two weeks later she sent me a $20 tithe. I figured he was good!

One man forgave and felt more prosperous and relaxed about work. He improved his relationships with his co-workers and his lover. Also, he felt he could express himself better. Financially it was his best month.

One lady, after forgiving, felt wonderful and achieved more clarity in her life. She also felt better about spending money on herself, plus she actually had more money to spend.

From all these definitions, I determined there are two categories of fortune: *"Fortunes of the Heart"* and *"Fortunes of the Pocketbook"*.

What keeps us from receiving these fortunes? We block ourselves from receiving our fortunes by the way we think, especially our unforgiving thoughts. The next chapter explores this principle in depth.

CHAPTER 3
RECEIVING FORTUNE

CHAPTER 4
THOUGHT IS CREATIVE

O riginally I heard the phrase "thought is creative" from Leonard Orr, but he was almost certainly not the first to have the idea, nor will he be the last. Many authors from the spiritual marketplace, motivational arena or New Thought churches agree with this concept.

Dr. Heather Anne Harder in her book, *Many Were Called, Few Were Chosen* states, "Life is a game created in the mind and brought into existence...to provide growth and joy."

Physicists agree that in order to develop something on the material plane, one must first create it in the mind.

SPEAK IT INTO EXISTENCE

We need language to translate our pictures and sensations into words, so we can more fully understand them and give them meaning.

Words are powerful, and the spoken word even more powerful. In the Bible, the universe was created from ideas and words: "And God said, 'Let there be light.'"

Many religious and mystical traditions explore the power of words and language. Prayers and incantations are used in religious and sacred rituals because words can manifest and create, protect and heal. Words can also hurt and destroy. Never underestimate the power of your words.

Helen Keller said she didn't even know of her own existence because she didn't have hearing or speech. When she was taught sign language, she became aware of herself. She signed herself into existence.

The basis of this book, the *Forgiveness equals Fortune* seminar and almost any self-awareness seminar on the market today is that we are responsible for our lives due to how and what we think.

The philosophy *that thought is creative* can be a freeing idea because it puts us in charge of our lives. Or the philosophy may be frightening, realizing we have attracted or created all people and events.

WHAT DO THOUGHTS DO?

Thought is language and pictures, feelings and sensations. In order for something to become manifest in material form, whether it be a building or a poem, it has to start as a thought, idea or picture in the mind.

Simply put: Positive thoughts produce positive results. Negative thoughts produce negative results. We can manifest and create fortune with loving, forgiving thoughts. Or we can destroy our lives, health, relationships and bank accounts with angry, resentful, judgmental thoughts.

Occasional random thoughts do not carry large amounts of energy and do not affect reality significantly. However, when our thoughts are accompanied by hefty amounts of energy, especially emotional, traumatic or highly creative energy, these thoughts may have a powerful effect upon our reality. When thoughts become conclusions and beliefs coupled with high energy, reality can be greatly affected.

Some neurological researchers say we have from 50,000 to 100,000 thoughts a day. We may not be aware of all of our thoughts. However, our thoughts, conclusions and beliefs are creating, whether they are conscious or unconscious. Our thoughts are producing results whether we are aware of the thought process or not.

Conclusions which have been made in childhood, at birth, in the womb, and perhaps even earlier, may be the foundation of our thought systems today. Many of those conclusions are negative and inaccurate. For example, a newborn may wake up in the hospital nursery and be hungry. He may cry to be fed. The nursery may be extremely busy and the nurse not able to take care of the child right away. The newborn could conclude, "I'll always be hungry," or "Nobody cares if I'm unhappy," or "My mother doesn't love me" - all of which are erroneous.

Conclusions are frequently based on misunderstood situations. Unfortunately, we continue to create and repeat those conclusions over and over again. As the newborn grew up, he might overeat, put on weight and perhaps later even develop high-blood pressure. His simple conclusion was "I'll always be hungry," which turned out to have serious consequences for the rest of his life. We must change our thoughts and beliefs in order to change our reality.

LIKE ATTRACTS LIKE (OR THOUGHTS ARE BOOMERANGS)

The Law of Electromagnetic Energy states: Whenever we create an electrical energy field (like a thought), simultaneously we produce a magnetic field or an *attraction* force.

Therefore, what we think about, we attract. Our thoughts are like boomerangs - they come back to us. Our visualizations have the power to affect our reality. When we visualize or think about something with all of our senses, we create a strong, electromagnetic field that attracts forces in the outside world to us. In other words, we will attract opportunities which will enable us to create exactly what we have been *thinking* about. Our brain, with the power of three-dimensional visualization, makes us self-fulfilling prophets. We become and create what we visualize, what we fear, what we think.

In my opinion, understanding the concept *thought is* creative and integrating it into our daily life is the basis of most self-improvement and self-awareness. This integration can change our reality from negative to positive. If we do not accept this theory, then we are a victim of fate, luck, circumstance and are at the mercy of others.

VICTIM RESPONSES

People respond to thinking they are victims in various ways. Below are listed some common responses, similar to those found in the Simons' Forgiveness book:

> *Ticked-off Timothy:* "You hurt me and I'm angry."

> *Vengeful Vicky:* "You hurt me and I'll get even with you." "You broke my heart so I'll break yours."

> *Doormat Dorothy*: "You hurt me and there's nothing I can do about it." Doormat People let other people walk all over them.

> *Pity Party Patty:* "I've been hurt before and I'll be hurt again." Sigh. "I'm always getting sick or losing money or friends, etc."

> *Martyr Martha:* "You've hurt me and I'm a far better person for it." "God must want me to suffer. Suffering is my lot in life."

> *Whining Willie:* "You hurt me and I'm gonna complain about it forever." Their words can feel like fingernails on a blackboard. "Why aren't you nice to me?"

Blaming Bart: "I've been hurt and you did it to me." Finger pointing may accompany this one. "The world is a mean place."

Over-indulging Oscar: "I've been hurt. Where's my bottle, my food, my drugs or my sex partner?" "My parents hurt me and I'm going to eat myself into oblivion."

Colin C. Tipping in his book, *"Radical Forgiveness"* says: "True forgiveness must include letting go of victim consciousness."

In conclusion, here is a humorous truth to lighten the mood: "To err is human. To blame it on someone else is even more human."

VICTIM - EXERCISE

Discover what thoughts are lurking in your mind. The following exercise will help to uncover some of those sinister thoughts, conclusions and assumptions.

I felt victimized when (describe in one sentence a major event in your life when you felt like a victim):

And I responded by becoming like (list which of the above characters you reacted like — Ticked-off Timothy, Doormat Dorothy, etc.):

For example:

I felt victimized when my car was stolen and vandalized.

I felt like Ticked-Off Timothy and Over Indulging Oscar - getting pissed-off and overeating or overworking, etc. Later I felt like Pity Party Patty.

THOUGHT IS CREATIVE

VICTIMIZED NOT VICTIM

When we accept the theory that our thoughts are creative, we are no longer victims. In other words, we take responsibility for the creation of all things in our lives. The next step is to recognize that we are being *victimized* by our thoughts. We only have to change our thoughts to change our circumstances. This is easy to say and sometimes not so easy to do.

Victimized is different than being a victim. Victimized means we are hurting and punishing ourselves by our creative thoughts, using other people as tools to accomplish this.

Other people are necessary in order to be a victim. I would sound pretty silly if I called 911 and said, "I just broke into my house and stole all my jewelry," or "Come quick, I need help. I just kidnapped myself."

When we believe other people are "doing it to us" and we blame them, we have forgotten we are the source of our reality. If your thoughts tell you someone else is to blame for the way your life is, you might want to stop trusting those thoughts. Jeff Foster says: "The mind is the ultimate in fake news."

When we accept our power, then we are source. People still seem to be "doing it to us," but we realize they are merely carrying out our subconscious and unconscious instructions and commands. Instead of being a victim, become the hero of your own story by forgiving and still have compassion for yourself and others who are dealing with a harsh reality.

THOUGHT SCRIPT

Other people are simply reflections of our thoughts and belief systems. These thoughts and belief systems are projected out into the Universe as *commands*. "People - hurt me!"

We then attract other people who are willing to carry out these unconscious instructions. Usually people who volunteer to do this have similar belief systems and lessons to learn that are enhanced by their participation with us. In consciousness, there are no victims – only volunteers and co-creators!

One method of becoming more aware of our thoughts is to jot down or type every thought we have. This can be very enlightening.

As we watch numerous angry, sad and unhappy thoughts parade through our minds, we discover why our reality may appear unfortunate at times. No wonder we have negative results.

Now that we know we are the source of our experiences, not victims, we have to deal with victimizing ourselves. When we interact with someone and we don't like what we've created, we can work together to discover which negative thoughts are producing the unpleasant results and change them.

The end result is two creative people, acknowledging their power, accepting total responsibility for themselves and no longer being the victim, or victimizer, of other people. From that position, there is no blame, there is no guilt, there is no judgment and forgiveness occurs naturally.

POWER TO THE PEOPLE

Understanding "thought is creative" puts us in charge, allows us to have control over ourselves and makes us the architect of our dreams. Whatever we can conceive of and believe, we can achieve. The more we accept this principle by noticing our realities and asking ourselves **"What thought or belief created this?"** the more we will see how our thoughts are affecting our reality. As we become adept with the process of noticing and discovering the thoughts behind our reality, we can then change our thoughts - thereby changing our reality. Dr. Norman Vincent Peale knew this back in the 1950s, teaching people how to *harness thoughts into the power of positive thinking.*

The acceptance of total responsibility may not be optional for adults. Whether we accept it or not, we are 100 percent responsible for every area of our life. This may be challenging to perceive because we see only in fragments rather than the whole picture of our lives and realities.

Over the years, I have watched people attempting to integrate this theory into their consciousness. At first they might say: "Yes, I create everything in my reality - except when my car was rear-ended." This is the famous "Yeah - but" response.

When people become more aware of their conscious and unconscious thoughts, they can see a connection between their reality and their thoughts.

THOUGHT IS CREATIVE

Since thoughts are creative, unforgiving thoughts of hurt, guilt, resentment, and hatred may return in the form of financial difficulty, pain, disease, relationship problems, unhappiness and a host of other unpleasant human conditions.

BEING SICK AND THOUGHTS

Dr. Deepak Chopra has formulated a theory based on modern neuro-chemical research. His theory roughly boils down to this: When we think certain thoughts, our brain secretes chemical neuro-transmitters, which then act on our brain, glands and organs, even influencing every cell of our body. Whether our system is activated or depressed depends on the kind of thinking we are doing.

Sickness can be used to get attention or love, to get sympathy, to get even with someone, to punish ourselves or to avoid people or situations. Sickness can also be used to slow us down and force us to rest. Sickness may be a reminder to think positively or practice forgiveness. When we discover the reasons for creating our illnesses, it is possible to stay healthier.

When using ill health for creative purposes, there are thousands of varieties of diseases and illnesses to use. When we have a need to be sick or feel a need to punish ourselves, we suppress our body's natural immune system with our negativity and allow the ever-present germs to invade the cells and make us sick.

We can take responsibility for our illnesses and discover what there is to learn from being sick. I do not mean to imply this is an easy task but rather merely offering a place to start.

HEAVEN AND HELL

Life consists of duality - positive and negative, right and wrong, pleasant and unpleasant, war and peace, love and hate.

Each quality has varying shades and flavors to it, going from the extreme of pure white light to the absence of light or darkness. Darkness feels like hell. Light is more enjoyable and feels like heaven.

Positive and negative are both the result of the mind, created by thoughts. Positive thoughts produce positive, heavenly results. Negative thoughts produce negative, hellish results.

GARBAGE DUMP

In all probability, we would not allow a truckload of garbage to be dumped in our living rooms - would we?

Yet most people allow negative, depressing, violent ideas and images to enter their psyches from the television, newspaper, social media and movies. We have gotten used to the negativity of pessimistic, turbulent news.

We have control over what we put into our mental computers. We should care as much about our own minds as we do our living rooms.

OTHER PEOPLE HAVE MENTAL COMPUTERS TOO

One day as I was walking through the park, I saw a mother and her two-year-old daughter. The mother had picked up the child and was brushing her off after falling down. I watched their interaction intently.

The mother spoke shrilly. "Be careful. You're always falling down and scraping yourself."

At that moment, the child took another step and began to fall again. The mother reached down, yanked the child up and said, "See. Didn't I tell you?" Not only was the mother helping to imprint the idea of falling down again, but gave the child who was learning to walk the impression that falling down was bad and would make her mother angry. That type of programming can be negative and harmful.

THE RUBBER BAND REMINDER

If you want to become more aware of your thoughts, get a rubber band and place it on your wrist. Every time you have a negative thought or judgment, stretch the rubber band away from your wrist and **gently** let it snap back.

When you snap your wrist, you will feel slight discomfort or pain. Most people have a tendency to move away from physical pain instinctively. As a result, you may focus more attention on changing or deleting your negative thoughts and judgments.

You may be quite surprised to discover how many negative thoughts and judgments your mind has. When you become aware of these thoughts and judgments, notice how they appear or manifest in your reality. You may be startled to see the connection.

Chapter 4
THOUGHT IS CREATIVE

CHAPTER 5
LIFE IS A STAGE

You have probably heard the famous quote from William Shakespeare, "All the world is a stage, and all the men and women merely players."

If the world is a stage and all human beings are the actors, then how life unfolds must be the script of our lives. Since we are the authors of our own lives, we must have written our life script exactly the way we wanted it to be, which means life is *perfect*.

The dictionary defines perfect as "whole, complete, accurate, with no parts missing."

When we say the Universe is perfect, we mean the Universe is a *complete* and *accurate* reflection of our consciousness, with everyone playing their part to perfection. Everyone and everything in our reality is a perfect reflection of our consciousness. Yes, people may have human flaws, but we are "perfectly flawed."

With this philosophy in mind, forgiving becomes easier. We are the director of our own stage play. We write the scripts, we cast the players and set the play in motion. Additionally, we are the captive audience.

Why sit in the audience and judge the players? They are only playing their parts the way we directed them.

Everyone in our stage play is performing their role perfectly, whether we are enjoying them or not. The villain who ties the girl to the railroad track is perfect. The landlord who evicts someone is perfect. The woman who runs into the back of our new car is perfect. These events may not be entertaining or joyous - but they are a perfect reflection of our consciousness and accurately reflect back our life scripts. Remember, thought is creative.

If we get evicted, the event is a direct result of our thoughts, either conscious or unconscious. The thought could be negative, like fear of homelessness. The thought could possibly be a positive desire, such as wanting a nicer home but unwilling or afraid to move. A thought existed first which created the situation.

COMPARING LIFE SCRIPTS

As we produce the stage play of our life, we observe others around us. Some people, we think, have better roles. Or we may think our roles are preferable. Someone else's script might seem more fun or easier. In the process of noticing whose life is better and whose is worse, we become involved in making judgment comparisons.

Since everything and everyone is perfect, we can accept ourselves as perfect too. When we accept ourselves the way we are, we have taken a step towards forgiving ourselves.

If **you** were to search the world over, would **you** be able to find anybody who is playing **you** better than **you** do? No matter what you are like - you are the best at being yourself. Anne Sermons Gillis in *her EZ Secret Newsletter* says:

> *"I've always wanted to be a star, so I tried out for the role of ME and got the part."*

When we accept ourselves the way we are, forgiveness can occur. Forgiveness is an acceptance of the way we are. John Newton in one of his free calls said:

> *"Accepting where we are includes accepting where we want to be. But we don't use where we want to be as a way of invalidating where we are."*

Here is a fascinating made-up word: "Flawsome" which means "someone who embraces their flaws, forgives themselves and knows they are awesome regardless."

Lauren, my dear friend and co-writer, was inspired to write the following story after taking the *Forgiveness equals Fortune* seminar. The "Rose and the Gladiola" is now part of her book, "Thymely Tales". The story is a light-hearted way of realizing how silly we are to compare ourselves to others.

THE ROSE AND THE GLADIOLA

Once upon a time in an old English garden there lived a Rose and a Gladiola. Their Garden was lovingly attended by the Gardener. He had spent his entire life gardening there. His father had been the gardener before him and had taught him everything he knew. He loved the Garden as if it were his own. He spent more time there than with his own family. His son was grown up now and assisted him. When he was no longer able to work, his son would take over the Garden.

The Gardener had put much time and care into the Garden. He collected scraps and peelings from Cook so he could mulch. In the fall, he carefully raked up every leaf and turned it over into the soil. From the dairy, he collected manure which he added liberally.

Consequently, the earth was rich in nutrients, loamy and dark. Whole generations of worms lived there with their families; their casings adding to the nutrients. Their burrowing improving the looseness of the soil, enabling plants to flourish.

The Rose and the Gladiola grew in this lush environment. No bugs were allowed to mar their appearance. The special soil encouraged them to grow large and beautiful. Their stalks were healthy and a deep color of green. Their blooms were full and soft. When the Gardener saw them, he would sigh in appreciation. They were both gorgeous, the Rose a pale pink, the Gladiola lemon yellow.

The Rose stood in the middle of the Garden, the warm sun shining down. The breeze ruffled her leaves. She looked over at the Gladiola, tall and proud, near the protection of the garden wall. "She could lean against the wall if she gets tired," mused the Rose. Rose started studying the Gladiola. "She is so nice and tall and elegant. Look how she sways in the breeze. Yellow is such a marvelous color. I wish I was tall and yellow."

The Gladiola became aware of the Rose's interest. "She sure is a pretty shade of pink. That looks so feminine. She's small and cute too. Being taller than most of the flowers here, I feel self-conscious and awkward."

"She's looking my way," said Rose to herself. "All of her blossoms are pointing in my direction. Wouldn't it be wonderful to have all those blossoms on one stately stem? They keep right on blooming, almost to the sky. That must be thrilling. I wish I had all those blooms."

"I feel so ugly next to that pretty pink Rose," murmured Gladiola. "I can smell her fragrance ALL the way over here. I wonder how I could get some of that perfume?"

"Oh, if only I didn't have all these awful thorns, I'd be a much better flower," complained Rose. "I don't want anyone to get hurt just by touching me!" She started to cry.

Gladiola couldn't look at the Rose anymore. "It's no good. She's a much better flower than me. Even a blind person could smell her. I have absolutely no perfume and I'm too tall. Even now I'm starting to fall over," she sniffed.

The Gardener walked into the Garden. He saw the Rose and the Gladiola drooped over. He walked over to them and asked with concern, "Whatever is the matter?"

They both told him their sad stories. Instead of feeling sad, the Gardener chuckled. "Well, my two beauties. This is an interesting dilemma. I suppose you want me to decide who is the best flower?"

"Yes, that would be wonderful!" They nodded in agreement.

"I can't," he stated simply. "You are both different and your beauty is unique as well. You're both perfect the way you are!" He touched each of them on their petals.

"You see, the miracle of life is variety," he continued. "Harmony and peace of mind will come to each of you when you realize that "different" is fantastic. Celebrate your differences!" With that he went to weed a different section of the Garden.

The Rose and the Gladiola smiled sheepishly at each other. Rose verbalized it for both of them. "Being me is magnificent, whether I'm a Rose, or a Gladiola, or even a Weed!" They closed their eyes in contentment and turned their leaves to the sun.

LIFE LIKE SCHOOL OR "YOU UNIVERSITY"

Once we accept we have created everything and that we are equal to everyone else, we can move forward - to realize that every person or situation in our life is a lesson. We can learn from every circumstance and relationship. Life is like school.

Let's call this school "You University." You go to the Universal campus and enroll in courses, like Relationships 101 or Finances 201 or After the Heart Attack 301. The difference between school and life is you forgot you enrolled. You get "enrollment amnesia."

Then the teacher arrives and class begins. Everyone in life could be considered your teacher because there are lessons to be learned in every situation. This statement was inspired by Florence Scovel Shinn in *The Game of Life and How to Play It*: "No one is your enemy; no one is your friend; every one is your teacher." However, once class begins, you immediately start judging and being upset with the teacher. Why get angry or upset? The teacher is just doing his or her job - the way everyone else is. When you live your life from this idea, life stops being such a struggle and becomes an adventure of classes, lessons and graduations.

Sometimes when I think of my life like school I feel like I received my Bachelors in Judgment and Resentment and now I'm getting my Masters in Forgiveness.

In daily life, when unpleasant or uncomfortable situations arise with other people, we need only to remember there is a lesson to learn and others are assisting us to learn it. If we can accomplish this, forgiveness is not needed. Forgiveness is only necessary when there is judgment or upset.

MIS-TAKE OR DIVINE DO-OVER

Since life is a play and we are players on the stage, sometimes we make mistakes by forgetting our lines, bumping into scenery or other actors or closing the curtain too quickly.

Because of that, we think others are better or "doing it" better than us. This comparison could cause us to think we are doing it wrong or making a mistake.

This is a more gentle definition of the word "mis-take." Mistake means "to re-do a scene." In the movies when doing a scene, they call it "take one." If there are mistakes, they do it again and call it "take two" and so on. If we do something we deem as wrong, we can just do it again. Rev. Michele Whittington at Creative Living Fellowship referred to this as a Divine Do-Over. Mistakes can be looked upon as opportunities to practice again and again until we feel "satisfied."

In fact, the most important part of learning is making mistakes. Mistakes actually help us to get to where we are going. Mistakes are part of taking baby steps until we grow up. Steven Spielberg didn't start out making Oscar-winning movies.

Below is a compassionate quote by an unknown author about mis-takes and lessons:

> "Never be defined by your past. It was a lesson - not a life sentence."

THE FOUR STEPS TO LEARNING

Learning is achieved in four stages:

1. *Unconscious Incompetence* - when we don't know what we don't know. Before learning to drive a car, we don't know how to start the engine, put the car in gear and drive it. All we can do is sit in the passenger seat, unaware of what propels or stops the vehicle.

2. *Conscious Incompetence* - the stage where we are beginning to discover what we don't know. We are taught about driving a car - starting, steering, braking, accelerating and shifting. We know what each pedal and knob is for but we use them awkwardly. We have to carefully think through each step in the driving process.

3. *Conscious Competence* - the stage of familiarity; becoming acclimated and comfortable. We are getting better at driving and can do several things at once, like turn the wheel, talk to a passenger, listen to the radio. Driving is becoming effortless and we don't have to think about each action so thoroughly anymore.

4. *Unconscious Competence* - the point at which we don't know what we know. We don't have to focus. We get in the car and drive without thinking about it. We drive automatically and naturally. If someone were to ask us how to drive, we would have to stop and think about what we know and what to show them.

Most mistakes are usually made in the second and third steps of learning. This is the place to do our "retakes" until we become *unconsciously competent.*

I was *unconsciously incompetent* in forgiveness before I met the woman who pointed out my inability to forgive. I didn't even know I needed to forgive. Then I moved into *conscious incompetence* when I realized how much I didn't know about forgiveness, how to forgive or even how much there was to forgive. All this however was gradually dawning on me. I made mistakes here and there and began practicing a great deal.

Then I shifted into *conscious competence*, began teaching others as well as myself, still making mistakes and adjustments and learning new processes leading to forgiveness. At some point, I became *unconsciously competent.* In the writing of this book, I had to recall, sometimes with difficulty, the knowledge I had accumulated.

THE ROCKET THEORY OF MISTAKES

A rocket or a missile gets to its goal, destination or target through the computer recognizing when it is "off course" and then firing its thrusters to adjust its trajectory. Being off course is how it stays "on course." The rocket's computer frequently makes errors and then corrects them, in order to reach the moon.

People are like rockets. Getting off course is part of learning, accomplishing a task or getting to a desired destination. Mistakes are the necessary, logical steps to learning and growing. Without judging our mistakes, we live in a state of forgiveness, accepting the natural process of life's lessons.

CHAPTER 6
RIGHT AND WRONG

Forgiveness takes us beyond the influence of judgments. Forgiveness often takes us to neutrality, beyond the realm of right or wrong, good or bad. If we recall the Horse Story at the end of the first chapter, the horse owner remained neutral about events happening in his life, while the town's people judged each event as either good or bad.

The story reveals two different methods of perceiving reality. Reality can be malleable, elastic and flexible beyond the veils of one's personal understandings, beliefs and experiences. Our certainty in the right/wrong philosophy of life can be a barrier or block to forgiving. Forgiveness has no right or wrong – it is neutral.

Andrew Hand states in his website article, *Neutrality: A Guide to Spiritual Centeredness*:

> *"Of all the things in life that we could be, neutral seems to be one of the least appealing. We are taught to be for things or against things. This is the way that society has socialized us. But what if it is in neutrality that you can move outside of your known perceptions and step into the realm of endless possibility? ...You aren't pulling or pushing, but merely standing still while moving along the track of life, waiting to receive all that you need from your source."*

THE NATURE OF NEUTRALITY

- Neutrality is the absence of:
  - positive or negative thinking;
  - right or wrong thinking;
  - good or bad thinking.
- Neutrality is the absence of bias, judgment or attachment to any particular outcome.
- Neutrality expresses no strong negative feelings.
- Neutrality is impartial and does not takes sides.
- Neutrality quiets the mind and rests peacefully in the present moment.
- Neutrality is an acceptance of what is.

CHAPTER 6
RIGHT AND WRONG

Neutrality is a skill that may be developed through forgiving, which allows us to exist in a state of peace and presence. By practicing forgiveness, we may find ourselves in the upbeat and tranquil realm of neutrality. Neutrality is when we express from our hearts no matter what another says or does.

Human beings often want to be right. We have been taught if someone is right – then someone else must be wrong. Even though we may appear to be right, it does not automatically follow that someone else is wrong.

ALTERNATE PERCEPTIONS OF REALITY

The visual illustrations below present alternate perceptions of reality while demonstrating that everyone seems to be right.

Stephanie sees and experiences the number 6.
Deborah sees and experiences the number 9.
Who is right? Who is wrong?

In this example, Nicole sees and experiences the letter "W," while Nigel sees and experiences the letter "M." In this instance, both people are correct from their own perspective. Both people have a different point of view – each one is **valid** and true for that person.

CHAPTER 6
RIGHT AND WRONG

In this illustration, there are a number of possible perspectives for each person. Laurie, Chet and Raleigh see the word "MOM," while Donya, Lonnie and Ruby see the word "WOW." Here is a list of other possibilities which may be perceived by each person:

- **Laurie:** "M" "MO" "OM" "MOM"
- **Chet:** "O" "MO" "OM" "MOM"
- **Raleigh:** "M" "OM" "MO" "MOM"
- **Donya:** "W" "WO" "OW" "WOW"
- **Lonnie:** "O" "WO" "OW" "WOW"
- **Ruby:** "W" "WO" "OW" "WOW"

Who's right and who's wrong? In these situations, there doesn't seem to be an absolute right or wrong answer. Each person appears to be right. Each perspective and viewpoint appears correct for that person.

Thus, when we shift our thinking away from duality, right versus wrong, good versus bad, black versus white, the world can be appreciated in an expansive, neutral way. Everyone's perception then is valid, which makes forgiving easier.

Some people are more perceptive than others; some people aren't paying attention at any given moment; others didn't notice what was happening because they were distracted by their own thoughts. These are some of the reasons witnesses to an accident or a crime will have as many different stories about what happened as there are witnesses. Eyewitness accounts therefore are considered the least reliable in a court of law.

Whenever possible, I am suggesting you remember that everyone may have a different "take" on reality, a different perception about an event, an occasion, or a simple phone conversation. During those times, it is helpful to remember that everyone's point of view is valid. You may both be right simultaneously.

When you let go of your attachment to a "right or wrong" viewpoint of life, then forgiving gets easier. If you are having difficulty forgiving someone, call to mind that they may see and experience life differently than you. A completely different perspective or point of view from yours is true and valid for them. Do your best to stay in a neutral state of forgiving.

BELIEF SYSTEMS AND REALITY

Our belief in right and wrong is just a belief system. I have offered these illustrations and ideas as a means to an end: To shift a belief system to end in forgiveness.

Also, please understand that I am attempting to share my ideas about reality in the simplest terms and in the fewest number of pages. Reality is quite complex and most likely beyond our human capacity to completely understand. As humanity, spirituality, and technology evolve, our belief systems change. Belief systems can be credible for a time and then discarded or upgraded. My suggestion is to focus on a belief system that moves you in the direction of compassion, forgiveness and love.

Lauren, my co-author, sent me this email: "Because of our work on this chapter over the past few days, a new poem appeared to me." Here is her poem which I find insightful, simple and profound.

**The Complete Idiot's Guide to Understanding
the Spiritual Universe
(in 25 words or less)
*by Lauren O. Thyme***

There is no reality with a capital R.
There is no truth with a capital T.
Everything is perfect, no matter what it looks like.

This chapter on Right and Wrong was designed to transform the way we think about: **"how we think."** The transformation of beliefs and thoughts enables us to remove blocks and barriers to our ability to forgive.

Another barrier to forgiveness is the emotions which accompany judgment, blame and criticism. To fully forgive, it is essential to release the emotions which prevent us from being at peace. The next chapter provides information, techniques and insight on how to deal with and manage emotions, allowing us to attain a more natural state of forgiveness.

CHAPTER 7
EMOTIONS

E motions are an inherent part of our make-up, our human heritage. All human beings experience emotions to one degree or another, both pleasant and unpleasant. Emotions are complex and often mysterious. Entire books have been written about emotions and how to cope with and/or release the unpleasant ones. This chapter presents a basic technique of releasing emotions – by feeling them. Forgiving would be easy if it was a mental process rather than emotional; however, Megan Feldman Bettencourt says:

> *"You can't think your way to forgiveness – you must feel your way."*

It is my experience that emotions exist to be felt and experienced. Also, it is their nature to flow and stay in motion, which means they want to be felt and then move on. One simple definition of emotion is 'energy in motion.' Forgiveness has the power to move and dissolve emotions from the body and mind, allowing our "fortunes" to then flow into our lives.

One of the most important steps in the forgiveness process is the willingness to meet, know and release deep emotions. Forgiveness often occurs naturally when we move through and release the judgmental emotions we are holding onto about ourselves, others or life situations. The more we are conscious of an emotion – the possibility of releasing it increases.

WHEN WE BURY OUR EMOTIONS, WE BURY THEM ALIVE!

Why bring up negative emotions and the past that created them? One reason is because usually it is not possible to go from anger, sadness, fear or any other negative emotion directly to forgiveness. When we forgive, we shift in the direction of compassion and love, which can move the unwanted emotions out of mind and body if we allow it. Compassion is a path to love or to update that phrase - a link to love.

Everyone has unpleasant or negative emotions at times. Many of us act unaffected, like we're **strong** and have got it all together. This "**cool**" act keeps our emotions suppressed and can prevent us from being emotionally authentic. As self-healing beings, sooner or later these unwanted emotions will emerge - whether we want them to or not and often when we least expect them. Boom – there they are!

Inner conflict is generated from the resistance to unwanted emotions. The Emotion says, "Feel me." The Person says, "No!" The emotion does not give up, so the internal conflict may amplify and gain power.

Many times discomfort and/or pain may be experienced with and from unpleasant emotions. No one wants to feel discomfort or pain, so we resist. We say "NO" I do not want to feel this – go away! This resistance to feeling emotions comes from fear. Feeling frightened of our emotions has been taught by parents to their children for thousands of years. The parents demonstrate their own relationship to emotions day in and day out. We may have learned that emotions are unacceptable or bad - sometimes receiving stern reprimands for feeling scared, angry or sad. Only recently people are becoming emotionally healthy. Previous generations could not teach what they did not know nor share emotional wisdom they did not possess.

How Much Does an Emotion Weigh?

Here is a story to demonstrate what is meant *by how much does an emotion weigh?* A little girl has an experience that warrants, let's say, an "ounce of sadness." She falls down, skins her knee, feels hurt and cries. In the midst of feeling her pain and emotion, she is interrupted by one of her parents: "You'd better stop that or I'll give you something to cry about!" And the little girl stops feeling and crying.

What did she do with the left-over ounce of sadness? She pushes it down and buries it within the cells of her mind and body.

Suppressed or unexpressed negative emotions make people act in ways that are out of proportion to current situations. Imagine the little girl grows up, accumulating 15 pounds of suppressed emotions along the way.

As an adult, a situation arises that calls for a half-pound of emotion. Instead of expressing the appropriate half-pound, the current situation stimulates all the feelings she has buried and stored up from childhood. She dumps the entire 15 pounds on the unsuspecting soul who unwittingly triggered her emotions.

Emotions don't die. They are simply buried deep in the recesses of our minds and bodies. Then they continue to demand expression or release in some form.

If we don't release a negative emotion, it haunts us, asking for satisfaction, wanting to be felt and then to move on. It's almost as if we hold our emotions prisoners inside of us. If the emotion is never acknowledged or allowed to be free, it demands even more of our attention.

Modern psychologists agree that suppressed emotions are often the basis of many diseases, illnesses, pain and other complaints. Popular self-improvement seminars and tools, as well as traditional therapy, address this critical issue of repressed emotions.

Suppressed emotions build up in the cells (or take up residence) and can become health problems, financial problems, and/or relationship problems. The emotion continues to demand to be felt, subtly wreaking havoc in our lives. Many times we are not aware that the source of our problems is our past, repressed emotions. When we forgive, these old suppressed emotions rise to the surface, giving us an opportunity to say hello as well as goodbye and allowing them to move through us.

If the cells are not cleansed by feeling the emotion or some other form of release, the problem can multiply. Stuck emotions can become so unhealthy that they have to be cut out with surgery or might even kill the body. To avoid this *unfortunate* sequence of events, feeling and forgiving may be preferable.

If we allow ourselves to address a negative emotion and feel it, then the emotion is appeased and "moves out." Sometimes merely shifting and acknowledging the feeling allows its release. In other words, the act of witnessing the emotions allows them to fade. Forgiveness emerges naturally from the willingness to feel our emotions fully, allowing them to stay in motion and move through us, without judgment. Appreciating and honoring every aspect of our being, especially our emotions, produces positive results.

This book is designed to clear problems in a simple and fun format. Next, you'll find several entertaining exercises to lighten your emotional load.

JUST LET GO - EXERCISE

While working on this 2nd edition of the *Forgiveness equals Fortune* book, I again started studying, researching and actively practicing, as well as sharing with others, the Forgiveness equals Fortune process. Once again I am amazed at how well the process works. My life has become quite delicious. For example:

- I'm letting people's love and acknowledgement in more.

- I'm able to naturally give more succinct, efficient and loving communications.

- Possibilities for more streams of income are showing up.

- I feel so much happier. (These are the *fortunes* I have received from actively forgiving.)

As part of my research, I enrolled in someone else's forgiveness seminar and have received value. It is truly wonderful for me to get to take a forgiveness seminar instead of leading one. I get the full benefit of being a student.

Forgiveness, of course, is about letting go – letting go of old grievances, letting go of judgments, letting go of blame, letting go of victim stories, letting go of the emotions standing in the way of true forgiveness. Being an emotional person, I have had people say to me: "Just let go, for goodness sakes." I would like to be able to do that. How is it done?

The inspiration for this simple exercise came from Sonia Choquette's On-line Forgiveness course, which conveys an experience of *just letting go*:

- Find an item that you like or use a lot - perhaps your keys, a remote or cell phone. Let this item symbolize or represent suppressed emotions.

- Standing next to a bed, sofa or padded chair, hold this item pressed up against your heart area – in the middle of your chest. Take a breath.

- Be aware of holding on. Now tighten your hold on the item and push it harder against your chest. Take a breath.

- ◆ Then open your hand and let what you are holding go. Let it drop. Notice how it feels to "just let go." Pay attention to how you feel after you have released it. Notice if there is any difference in the way your hand feels. Do you feel any difference in your heart area? Do you feel an emotion of loss or concern?

- ◆ Repeat this several times, breathing and noticing any feelings. When you release your object, does it feel like something is missing? Do you feel slightly uncomfortable? Does it feel a little scary? Or do you feel relief? Do you feel lighter or happier?

- ◆ Each time you drop the item, notice the sensations in your body and experience the release. Do the exercise until you can sense how easy letting go can be.

In your daily life when you find yourself having difficulty letting go of a challenging emotion, recall this exercise. Recall the feelings you experienced when "letting go" of your personal item. Take a breath and remember letting go being easy.

My friend, Anne Sermons Gillis, wrote a wonderful book called, "EZosophy." Simply put, she writes that life can be easy – or at least easier. Anne says in her newsletter "The EZ Secret Newsletter":

> "Learn to live in the flow. There's no business like flow business."

ANGER

Even though anger is one of the most commonly-felt emotions, many of us tend to be frightened of its intensity. Below is a pertinent quote from Codependent No More.

> "Unpleasant feelings are like weeds. They don't go away when we ignore them; they grow wild and take over. Our angry feelings may one day come roaring out. We say things we don't mean. Or, as usually happens, we may say what we really mean. We may lose control and unleash ourselves in a fighting, spitting, screeching, hair-pulling, dish-breaking rage. Or we may do something to hurt ourselves. Or, the anger may harden into bitterness, hatred, contempt, revulsion, or resentment."

Anger is most dangerous when it is suppressed. If suppressed for extended periods of time, anger grows and then erupts into rage. Rage is the behavior accompanying suppressed anger - the releasing of the emotion into action or expression.

TANTRUM - EXERCISE

There are dramatic or more confrontational ways to deal with our suppressed anger. One of these is called the "tantrum."

A child instinctively knows how to process emotion by expressing it in a very physical way. Unfortunately, most parents are not thrilled about tantrums and usually will squelch a child's natural tendency to experience and release emotions. As adults, we too want to release anger. Isn't that what we do by yelling at the kids, driving too fast or slamming the door when we're angry?

A conscious adult tantrum can be fun, good exercise and productive. Colin Tipping in his book *"Radical Forgiveness"* says "Anger is very effectively released through the combination of physical action and the use of the voice." A successful tantrum doesn't have to last very long. This is how it can be done:

- ◆ Lie down, face up, on your bed by yourself.

- ◆ Think about someone or something you're angry about and breathe deeply. This exercise works even better if you're already angry.

- ◆ Kick your legs like you're swimming fast. Breathe.

- ◆ Pound your fists into the bed, like you are hitting the person you're angry with. Take a deep breath.

- ◆ Grab a pillow and shout obscenities into it and breathe. Conscious breathing is imperative. Breathing forces emotion to the surface by pumping it up and out, allowing the anger to be more easily released.

- ◆ If you feel like you have released all you can lying on your back, turn over on your hands and knees and pound on your pillows and mattress, breathing hard through the mouth if possible.

- ◆ After you are either drained or exhilarated, lie down on your back again, relax your entire body and breathe. Notice how you feel.

If you perform the tantrum exercise before you discuss an emotionally-charged problem with another person, you may find your conversation calmer, rather than a battle or a shouting match.

Recently, I discovered that this tantrum exercise can not only disarm anger but also release sadness or any other feeling you are not enjoying. I felt some low-grade sadness the other day, and I started kicking and pounding on my bed. The sadness got "kicked out" of my body and cleared my mind. I felt so much better. See if it works for you.

Swami Beyondananda, a metaphysical comedian, calls this practice **"tantrum yoga."** He says when you master it - you can then use your anger to heat your home in the winter!

SURFACE AND DEEP EMOTIONS

While teaching forgiveness seminars in Las Vegas, Nevada, in the mid-1980's, I was introduced to a system of identifying emotions that helped me understand myself and other people in a unique way. Dr. Kenneth Fabian, a psychiatrist living in Las Vegas, developed a theory that emotions can be divided into two categories – **surface** and **deep** emotions.

SURFACE EMOTIONS

In Dr. Fabian's system, the term **surface** refers to location and means **on top**. These emotions are lying on top of, covering up and protecting us from feeling the deeper emotions which lie underneath.

Below is a list of the cover-up surface emotions. These are divided into categories or groups. They can be similar in nature and seem to be related or belong to the same family of emotions:

- **The Anger Group**: annoyed, bored, frustrated, irritated, angry, resentful, rage, spiteful, vengeful.

- **The Anxiety Group**: agitated, anxious, bitter, humiliated, insecure, panic, worried.

- **The Guilt Group**: envious, greedy, guilty, lust, regret, remorse, shame

- **The Pride Group**: arrogant, conceited, pity, pride, triumphant

- **The Feeling Good Group**: acts happy when not, giddy, falls in love too often, too quickly or too easily.

We may use all of these groups to a certain extent, but it is common for people to have one favorite group they use to distract themselves from their deep emotions - with perhaps a back-up group. I personally use the Anger Group with a back-up of Anxiety. Which groups do you use?

DEEP EMOTIONS

For this system, the term **deep** refers to location, as well as lying **deep** below a layer of surface emotions. These deep emotions are tender, vulnerable and make us feel defenseless like a child. Deep emotions represent the original emotions from past experiences which we want to side-step. Most people are ill-prepared to deal with their tender emotions. We have avoided them by stuffing the deep feelings down and hiding them underneath the surface emotions. We hid them away, so we didn't have to deal with them and the subsequent pain they evoked. Furthermore, we have been constantly struggling to avoid or ignore them ever since.

To truly forgive, it is the **deep** emotions which are the most vital to feel and heal. They are the emotions which are standing in the way of true forgiveness.

Below is a list of some deep emotions – the ones we do our best to avoid. These are the tender, shy, vulnerable, painful emotions that can be more challenging to feel:

- ◆ sadness, grief, lonely
- ◆ hurt, rejected or used, abandoned
- ◆ embarrassed, humiliated, shame
- ◆ fear, horror, terror
- ◆ helpless, hopeless, trapped

We tend to avoid, protect and distract ourselves from these emotions. The reason we want to disregard our **deep** emotions is because we are afraid to be vulnerable and defenseless, feelings often stemming from our childhood experiences. Few role models exist in our society that demonstrate how to be defenseless. Therefore, most people use their **surface** emotions to avoid the unfamiliar, scary, defenseless feelings. Surface emotions act like an emotional by-pass system.

Once you become aware of your protective emotions, you can acknowledge their presence and then allow yourself to dive below the surface emotions into the deep emotions. Surface emotions act like signals that a deep emotion may need to be explored. In other words, when you find yourself experiencing a surface emotion, you can tune in and ask what is really going on, what are you avoiding, or what is being covered up? Then just meet that deep emotion and get to know it. Say "hello" and notice how it feels. Remember to breathe and let your breath move the emotion up and out.

This system of emotional identification will show you how to stop wasting time processing surface emotions when the deep emotions are actually the ones blocking you from true forgiveness and your fortunes of the heart and fortunes of the pocket book.

PLEASANT DEEP EMOTIONS

Here's some good news. There are pleasant deep emotions as well, wanting to be felt and acknowledged. Below is a list of these more appealing deep emotions:

- relieved, curious, surprised
- contented, carefree, happy, joyful
- grateful, wonder, detached, serenity
- mastery, awe, bliss

Practice noticing when you feel relief, curiosity or surprise. These emotions come up quite a bit in life, but rarely do we pay attention to them. In fact, take a moment right now and recall a time when you felt **relieved**. Notice if you feel tender and vulnerable. Take a deep breath please.

Whenever possible, notice, acknowledge and focus upon the feelings of contentment, happiness or joy as they arise. Remember, what you focus on expands. The more we focus on the pleasant emotions, the more pleasant we feel. After all, aren't these the emotions most everyone wants to experience in life? If that's what we want, then practicing is logical.

Before learning this list of emotions, I never considered "mastery" an emotion. So now whenever I do something really well, I notice how it feels and I allow myself to sink into and enjoy the feeling of mastery.

This Emotional Awareness System, now called EAS (pronounced ease), is about becoming aware of and managing emotions. When you are aware of the difference between **surface** and **deep** emotions, you can successfully handle and make peace with your emotions. Then you can focus your attention on feeling the **pleasant deep** emotions of contentment, gratitude, wonder, mastery and awe. Sounds like a great plan to me!

A WELL OF EMOTION - EXERCISE

You can access a deep emotion by imagining yourself going down into a deep well, which is a subtle way to process your vulnerable feelings. Take one step down into the well of the emotion, noticing how it feels and merely "being with" the emotion. Once you are comfortable, drop a little lower into the emotion, breathing and noticing. If it gets too uncomfortable, come up and out of the feeling.

Next drop down into the emotion again, this time going lower. You do not have to drop to the bottom of the well of emotion all at once. Take one little chunk at a time. But keep dropping down into the emotion and feeling it. Each time you do, a little bit of the emotion dissipates. If you practice this often enough, the unpleasant emotions will dissolve.

Once you come out of the well, a layer of the emotion will have disappeared because: emotions want to be felt and to keep moving.

Perhaps in the deep, hidden levels of this well of emotions, we will find the pleasant deep emotions like joy, awe and wonder. Swami Beyondananda, a very wise spiritual comedian, has this to say about the well of emotions:

> "Underneath all the stress and distress and sadness of life is a deep well of joy, and every time laughter bubbles up from this deep well, we experience deep wellness."

BROKEN TEACUPS AND SPIRITUALLY BLIND - EXERCISE

Imagine you are an antique collector. You've been collecting a set of teacups for fifteen years. Two cups and saucers are missing. A friend calls one day and says, "I believe I saw your teacups down at the antique store on Main Street."

Excitedly you rush down to the antique store. It's true. The cups and saucers are on display and cost $200. You are thrilled because their purchase completes your fifteen-year process of collecting.

As you walk home with your cups and saucers, you turn a corner, and a man bumps into you. You and the sack containing the cups and saucers fall to the concrete. They smash into a million pieces. As you angrily get up, you notice the man who bumped into you is carrying a white cane. The person who destroyed your beautiful cups is *blind*.

Is it easier to forgive the man because he's blind? Or are you still angry? How would you feel if the person was a reckless teenager or a business man rushing to a meeting?

> *"People who are not loving or positive are blinded by repressed emotions and cannot see where they are going. If we remember everyone has moments of spiritual blindness, forgiveness becomes simple. We can tell ourselves "Oh, well, it wasn't his fault. He couldn't see me.*
>
> *Remember, your creative thoughts and suppressed emotions have helped to create situations. Perhaps an event is a reflection of your own blindness. Maybe you are unable to truly allow yourself to have what you desire."*

GUILT

Although we are not victims of circumstance or other people, we can be victimized by our own guilty beliefs. And *guilt demands punishment*. If we feel guilty, we create a script for other people to punish us.

Punishment comes in many forms: monetary problems, disease, pain, relationship turmoil, never getting what we want, low self-esteem, lack of sexual fulfillment, compulsive behavior and addictions - all sorts of "broken teacups."

LOVE

Love is our natural state of being. Once we allow ourselves to experience and release both our surface and deep feelings, we cleanse our emotional self. When our emotional self is clean, then our natural state of love returns, bringing with it joy, ecstasy, serenity and other life-enhancing emotions. The return to the natural state of love explains why fortunate things happen when people take the *Forgiveness equals Fortune* seminar. Other natural states of being are: awe, carefree-ness, contentment, forgiveness, gratitude, happiness, intimacy, mastery, self-acceptance, wonder, innocence and patience.

One of the most important steps in forgiving is the release of the emotions standing between you and forgiveness. Otherwise, we experience only "intellectual forgiveness." It is time to shift from the head to the heart. Andrew Bennett said: "The longest journey you will ever take is the 18 inches from your head to your heart." When we make that shift, peace and love will be our reward. This is a quote from Rumi, a 13th century poet and Sufi mystic:

> *"Your task is not to seek for love, but merely to seek and find all of the barriers within yourself that you have built against it.."*

WHY BOTHER?

People ask me, "But if my natural state is love, why should I bother feeling and releasing my negative emotions?" This is a good question and one that deserves an answer. Melody Beattie in "Codependent No More" says:

> *"The big reason for not repressing feelings is that emotional withdrawal causes us to lose our positive feelings. We lose the ability to feel. Sometimes, this may be a welcome relief if the pain becomes too great or too constant, but this is not a good plan for living. We may shut down our deep needs - the need to love and be loved - when we shut down our emotions. We may lose our ability to enjoy sex, the human touch. We lose the ability to feel close to people, otherwise known as intimacy. We lose our capacity to enjoy the pleasant things in life."*

When we do not experience our emotions, they accumulate within us. Suppressed emotions can be creative as well, just as thought is creative. The energy of the repressed emotions vibrates out into the universe. Then the universe presents us with situations which force us to feel that particular emotion. If we continue to resist or avoid the emotion, more situations will arise necessitating the feeling of that emotion in order to heal.

When we become comfortable with all of our emotions, we can allow them to move through our body like a wave of energy, passing right through. When we resist, the wave crashes down on our heads. Emotional awareness and release is the key to peace and the ability to create what you want in your life.

HURT IS LIKE DIRT

Forgiveness has many levels. Resentment and hurt are like dirt, while forgiveness is similar to cleaning your house. The first cleaning removes the top layer of dirt and makes the house fit for guests. With the second cleaning, you may notice dirt on the blinds and under the furniture. So you move the furniture, vacuum and dust, and the house gets cleaner. Then you realize the walls have lost their brightness so you repaint, and the house begins to sparkle.

Please be patient with your forgiveness process. Acknowledge each cleaning for its effectiveness and keep going. Cleaning or forgiving brings awareness to the next level of dirt/hurt which leads you to a new level of cleaning/forgiving.

As we clean up negative emotions, we stop creating events which stimulate those feelings. Releasing our emotions voluntarily is sensible in order to avoid recreating unpleasant situations, which force us to feel. As we consciously and fearlessly move through our emotions, a wonderful thing starts to occur. We begin to experience pleasurable emotions like joy, bliss and serenity as energy flows unimpeded through our bodies.

ANCESTRAL FORGIVENESS

Geneticists and other scientists studying epigenetics now believe that traumas of our ancestors may attach to their DNA and be passed onto future generations. Consequently, they think it is possible that we may experience the stress and strain of our forebears' emotional experience in our bodies.

Can you imagine the excruciating experiences our ancestors might have endured in just the last five hundred years? For example: war, famine, economic collapse, tragic or painful death, physical, emotional and sexual trauma, etc. Forgiving our lineage may be a wise thing to do for our own healing and peace of mind, as well as that of the planet. After all, what could it hurt?

OTHER LIFETIMES

A poll which was conducted by a global research company, Ipsos for Reuters News, finds that approximately half the world's population believes in some form of after life, past lives and/or reincarnation.

One of my favorite teachers, Sal Rachele, who is a mystic, clairvoyant, and successful author, has this to say about other lifetimes in his Article "Past, Parallel and Simultaneous Lifetimes:

> *"The subject of other lifetimes is a vast area of mystery to many. It used to be that people thought of other lifetimes as part of a linear progression taking place in linear time. From a higher dimensional perspective, all lifetimes are occurring simultaneously in both space and time, making them parallel rather than past in nature.*

> *My favorite metaphysical analogy is the movie. The reel contains all time - past, present and future. But we play it a frame at a time and it seems like a linear progression. Quantum physics tells us that reality "blinks" on and off millions of times a second - see the correlation? It gives the appearance of relative motion - the definition of "time". The mind is the projector and the screen is third dimensional life."*

I also like what my co-author, Lauren O. Thyme, said: "No one knows anything for sure. There is no truth with a capital T. Our ideas, theories and learning are always in flux – always changing and expanding."

If a possibility exists that we are living simultaneous lives, we can use quantum forgiveness affirmations like:

- ◆ I totally and completely forgive myself for any negative thoughts, words or actions from any lifetime, any dimension, or any timeline. I am forgiven now and forevermore.

One of my favorite affirmations is:

- ◆ I forgive and cancel out any negative thought, word or deed I have experienced in any lifetime, any dimension, any timeline; and I affirm that only my positive thoughts, words and deeds manifest in my reality. Thank you.

This is a simple ancestral clearing prayer inspired by John Newton:

"Infinite Creator: Please help me, all my family members, all our relationships, all our ancestors and all their relationships throughout all time, throughout all lives - to forgive all hurts and wrongs whether physical, mental, emotional, spiritual, sexual or financial. Please lift the pain, burden, debt, negativity and limitations of any kind and transform them into love and peace, now and forevermore. Thank you."

I forgive myself and all my ancestors to the beginning of time - just in case!

To lighten the topic, here is a little past life humor: "I personally don't believe in past lives. However, I might in my next life."

GRIEVANCES AND ILLNESSES

Life-threatening and/or painful illnesses are complex and complicated, both in the treatment, as well as the origin. Forgiving past grievances is a powerful place to start your healing process. Becoming aware of and releasing any emotions you may be holding or storing in your body is a formidable approach to natural healing - through forgiveness. Often what may stand in the way of complete forgiveness are emotions we have avoided or suppressed in the past. Unfortunately, when we "bury our emotions, we bury them alive." Emotions often seek expression and resolution in unpleasant ways, such as illness. Forgiveness has the power to heal. You can test it for yourself.

FORGIVENESS WORKOUT

Forgiving is like a workout. You can do your exercises at the Forgiveness Gym. Some people go every day; some go three or four times a week; some once a week; some once a month. Some people don't work out at all. When you do your forgiveness exercises, you eliminate grievances from your mind and body.

This is a question I sometimes ask myself: "How much does a grudge weigh and how many grudges am I carrying?" I prefer to live my life free of grievances and grudges – so I forgive whenever I remember. When you do your exercises, you may come to appreciate the beauty and power that forgiveness brings.

A forgiveness workout is easier when you have a forgiveness coach. With a coach, you can become a *Forgiveness Olympian*. If you are interested in pursuing forgiveness as an in-depth clearing exercise, you can email me at the address on the last page under Forgiveness Support.

FORGIVENESS SUCCESS CONSCIOUSNESS

Whenever I do forgiveness work, I pay close attention to what happens in my life for the next week to ten days. The moment something good happens – I label it a forgiveness success. Maybe there is a direct correlation – maybe there isn't. But since I am building a Forgiveness Success model, I choose to call it a success.

Writing down the good that comes after forgiving is a powerful way to build your forgiveness success consciousness. One of my clients called this written journal "The Log of Positive Happenings," which you can refer back to later. From my experience, forgiveness is quite rewarding when I am willing to look inside and forgive myself, as well as forgive others. So now we are ready to move onto the *Forgiveness equals Fortune* seminar.

CHAPTER 7
EMOTIONS

CHAPTER 8
THE SEMINAR

TEACHING WHAT I MOST NEED TO LEARN

The *Forgiveness equals Fortune* seminar has been an outgrowth of my own desire to learn how to forgive. Since forgiving was difficult for me, I had to research it thoroughly in order to integrate it into my life. I then worked with others to find effective techniques. After many years of conducting seminars, I am ready to share what I learned with you and learn more for myself. Teaching is learning twice.

People taking my Forgiveness seminar experience powerful, positive results very quickly. I sometimes laugh when I think of the positive results I could have produced for myself had I been able to take the *Forgiveness equals Fortune* seminar as many times as I led it.

THE ORIGINAL SEMINAR

The purpose of the original *Forgiveness equals Fortune* seminar:

> *"To experience the release of thoughts and emotions which block forgiveness and then to experience our ability to receive good fortune."*

Following are the basic processes of the *Forgiveness equals Fortune* seminar. Before you start, please read the brief directions below.

1) Allow an adequate amount of time to do each exercise without being interrupted.

2) You may want to read through the Forgiveness equals Fortune seminar chapter, returning later to do the exercises.

3) Spaces are provided in the book to write answers; however, you may want to use a separate pad of paper.

4) Remember to take deep breaths on a regular basis, as well as breaks to relax and integrate the information.

AFRAID TO FORGIVE - EXERCISE

The two exercises below will help you discover blocks or barriers you may have to forgiving. Make a list of the reasons you are afraid to forgive.

"One of the reasons I am afraid to forgive is . . . "

✻

✻

✻

✻

Some common reasons people are afraid to forgive are:

- ◆ I'll be vulnerable.
- ◆ I'll get hurt again.
- ◆ I'll have to admit I was wrong.
- ◆ I'm weak.
- ◆ I will feel pain.
- ◆ I'll lose control or power.
- ◆ They'll do it to me again.

The most common fear is the *fear of being vulnerable*, that the problem or situation will repeat itself and we will be hurt again. Paradoxically, when we do not forgive, then the lesson remains unlearned, and the unpleasant situations may keep repeating. When we forgive, the lesson completes itself and the problem disappears - unless deeper forgiveness is needed.

REASONS I DON'T WANT TO FORGIVE - EXERCISE

Complete this sentence and make a list of the reasons you do not want to forgive:

"One of the reasons I don't want to forgive is . . ."

✸

✸

✸

✸

Common reasons people don't want to forgive are:

- ◆ I want to be right.
- ◆ I want the other person to feel bad and guilty.
- ◆ I/they should be punished.
- ◆ I/they don't deserve to be forgiven.
- ◆ What would I do without my guilt?
- ◆ I wouldn't have anything to talk about.
- ◆ It is easier to stay angry.
- ◆ I am used to life being this way. Change would be too scary.
- ◆ I might experience too much pleasure or success in my life.

The most common reason people don't want to forgive is that *they want to be right*. To forgive might mean we have been wrong all along. Forgiveness accepts all points of view as valid. Every person's perception is true for them, even if it doesn't match anyone else's picture. Refer back to the illustrations in the chapter on Right and Wrong.

When we live from the belief there is a right and a wrong, someone will **be wrong**. Forgiveness eliminates right and wrong. Forgiveness respects that **everyone's perception is valid and therefore not wrong.**

PEOPLE TO FORGIVE - EXERCISE

Make a list of the people, organizations and/or groups you want or need to forgive. If you are not sure forgiveness is necessary, recall the exercise where you think about someone you resent or feel hurt by. Then notice how you feel. If you feel uncomfortable, your jaw tightens, your breath shallows, or you feel a pain in your solar plexus/belly, or anywhere else in your body, add that person, organization or group to your list.

When making your list, be sure to take a deep breath after each one. Breathing keeps the energy and emotions moving up and out of the mind and body.

Your mother, your father and your self will probably be at the top of the list. I call this the *Forgiveness Trinity* since forgiving all three is basic to freeing yourself. If you were adopted, had step-parents and/or lived in a foster home, your list will be longer.

Also list present-day spouses, business partners, ex-spouses and ex-business partners. Children and siblings are also a good choice for your list. You may want to list God as well.

In addition, you may list groups of people, such as men, women, doctors, nurses, churches, Republicans, Democrats, multi-level marketing companies and bankers. Some people need to forgive inanimate objects such as their cars, computers, bank accounts, televisions and other mechanical devices.

Have any of you ever cursed your body because it was too tall, too short, too thin, too fat, or didn't work properly? If yes, then list your body.

Isn't it amazing how many people and things there are to forgive?

LIST OF PEOPLE TO FORGIVE

*

*

*

*

*

*

*

*

*

*

*

*

*

*

CHOOSE SOMEONE - EXERCISE

The second part of this exercise is to put a star (★) by the person, group or object you want to start forgiving.

Most likely, people who you are currently having problems with will draw your attention. If you like, start with them. Many times, when forgiving others, you may find you must switch over to someone from The Forgiveness Trinity - yourself, your mother or your father. Just be aware as your thoughts and feelings come up - they may lead you to deeper levels of hurt or upset from childhood. This is a good thing. You might as well focus on the core issues that need forgiveness.

When choosing someone to forgive, rely on your Inner Guidance. At one level, it doesn't really matter where you start as long as you commit to forgiving yourself and your parents at some point. The foundation of most blocks to receiving fortunes are the grievances, grudges, resentments and hurts from this Trinity. The entire next chapter is devoted to Forgiving Yourself.

After you feel complete with the Trinity, continue on with other significant relationships where forgiveness is needed. Let yourself think of the person. If you find they cannot walk safely through your mind without stirring up feelings or upsets, this is another sign encouraging forgiveness.

The *Forgiveness equals Fortune* book is a Workbook. You will be amazed at your results if you take the action necessary to forgive. Some people are really good at working by themselves and learning. For me, I learn easier if someone shows me the way the first time. If you would like some forgiveness coaching to jump start the process, please connect with me.

Perhaps one way to effectively do this forgiveness work is to first read through the instructions. After the visualization, you will find a simplified version of the *Forgiveness equals Fortune* method which you may use.

THE CREATIVE BLAME PROCESS

In the Creative Blame Process, the goal is to formulate a list of everything you want to forgive a person for.

In this process, you will list your negative thoughts, which could generate unpleasant sensations and emotions in your mind and body. You'll have a great opportunity in this exercise to discover and release your feelings.

When you are making your list, be very specific. Do not put down generalities. Politeness doesn't particularly work in this exercise. Be sure to get "down and dirty." Using four-letter words is helpful, as well. If using obscenities supports you to heal anger and resentment, then being **prudish** would be **foolish**.

If you list something like, "Husband, I resent you for lying," get specific about the lie. "Husband, I resent you for lying about your affair with your secretary."

Be sure to allow time after this last process for the positive counter part of the Creative Blame Process, which is the Forgiveness Process. **These two processes should be done consecutively**. It is not wise to write negative sentences without doing the forgiveness exercise immediately.

THE CREATIVE BLAME PROCESS - EXERCISE

Choose one person from your list you want to forgive. Then place their name in the following sentences. Do these sentences in any order. The important thing is to stimulate your mind to bring up any emotions, thoughts and memories which are stored away.

Go as far back in your mind and life as you can remember and list your grievances. It is not necessary to rewrite the beginning of each sentence. Start by writing "for" or "about" and then the "judgment."

.... I'm angry at you for ....
Name   **Judgment**

.... I hate you for ....
Name   **Judgment**

.... I feel afraid about ....
Name   **Judgment**

.... I feel sad about ....
Name   **Judgment**

.... I feel guilty about ....
Name   **Judgment**

In your mind, say the first part of the sentence and then listen to your mind's judgmental response. Write the judgment down.

Be sure to take a deep breath after every sentence you write. If you are not breathing deeply, you could be subtly holding your breath as well as holding onto the grievance.

If you have emotions surface while doing this process, let them come up and breathe them out. Tears will help to cleanse emerging emotions.

Breathe in what you want:	Forgiveness.
Breathe out what you don't want:	Emotions like hurt, sadness, resentment, etc.

If you run out of grievances, use other forms of that person's name. For instance, you might have called your mother "mommy" when you were small or you may have used her given name as an adult.

Cleansing visualization: When you are doing this process, visualize the grievance rising up from the subconscious mind to the conscious mind. Then watch the grievance flow out the end of your pen or pencil onto the piece of paper.

The first part of the *Forgiveness equals Fortune* process will be directed towards **Mother** and **Father**. Later we will address Forgiving the **Self**.

Grievances commonly held against Mother:

- for not loving me; for ignoring me
- for criticizing me; for mocking me, for lying to me
- for being cranky or irritable; for verbally abusing me
- for hurting me; for hitting me; for slapping me
- for not breast-feeding me; for not cooking
- for acting helpless, manipulative or controlling
- for smothering me; for being jealous of me
- for leaving dad/me

Grievances commonly held against Father:

- for not being physically or emotionally available
- for not expressing your feelings
- for not telling me you love me
- for not touching, hugging or kissing me
- for spanking or punishing me
- for being mean; for being angry; for being an alcoholic
- for working too much; for rarely being home
- for abandoning us

ANYONE ELSE? - EXERCISE

After you finish this list, go back and re-read each grievance. Notice if you are holding those particular grievances towards anyone else in your life. For example, you may be holding grievances against yourself, one of your parents or your spouse for the same thing. If so, place their name or initials at the side of the grievance. Go down the whole list and put a name or initials beside every common grievance.

Look back then and see if there is a pattern. For instance, if the original list specifies grievances against your mother - and your initials show up beside most of those judgments, you can see the pattern emerging. Your mother is reflecting back your thoughts about yourself. YIKES.

If your original list has grievances towards your father and your husband's initials show up predominantly at the side, guess what? You married a man who will support you to forgive your father by reflecting similar personality traits.

The first time you see these grievance patterns can be somewhat disturbing. The more you notice the connection between people and their common grievances the easier to accept that life is a reflection of who you are, what you think and what you do. Seeing and accepting this leads us to the power of taking full responsibility for our lives and releases us from the negativity of blaming others. This initialing process can be very enlightening. Please take note.

FORGIVENESS PROCESSES

Now it is time to forgive. If you have just done the Creative Blame Process, **be sure** to use one of these methods of forgiving **immediately**. Don't put it off and say you'll do it later. Please do it right now – unless you decide to do all the processes after reading the instructions.

WRITING FORGIVENESS AFFIRMATIONS

One method of forgiveness is to take each one of the grievances you listed above and write a forgiveness affirmation. You may also type your forgiveness affirmations on your computer.

An affirmation is a positive thought you immerse in your consciousness to produce a desired positive result. Some people resist writing or saying a certain affirmation because it seems like a lie. Affirmations are lies, until you work with them long enough, and they become true. Once an affirmation becomes true, you usually stop working with it. The reason we work with affirmations is to make them true for us. I'm sure you have heard that if you tell a lie long enough, you begin to believe it. Usually that statement only applies to the negative aspect of lying. Affirmations are the positive aspect of lying or saying something that isn't true in the moment but your intention is for it to become true.

I FORGIVE YOU FOR ... Examples:

- ◆ Mother, I forgive you for hurting me.
- ◆ Mommy, I forgive you for not loving me.
- ◆ Mom, I forgive you for leaving Dad.
- ◆ Mama, I forgive you for criticizing me.

EASIER FORGIVENESS AFFIRMATIONS

If you find using **"I forgive you for…"** is too hard to do, you may have to take a step back and write, type or say out loud an easier forgiveness affirmation - working your way up to "I forgive you for…"

To make the forgiveness affirmation easier, write:

I'M WILLING TO CONSIDER FORGIVING YOU FOR ...

"Mother, **I'm willing to consider forgiving you for…**"

Write the "I'm willing to consider forgiving" affirmation until you feel more comfortable and can move on. Then write:

I'M WILLING TO FORGIVE YOU FOR ...

"Mother, **I'm willing to forgive you for….**"

Write this a few times until it becomes comfortable. After working with these easier forgiveness affirmations, once again return to the original forgiveness affirmation:

I FORGIVE YOU FOR ...

"Mother, **I forgive you for**…." Notice if it is now easier to write this affirmation.

Do this forgiveness process on each grievance listed. Remember to take an occasional deep breath. After writing numerous forgiveness affirmations per grievance, then write:

I TOTALLY AND COMPLETELY FORGIVE YOU NOW.

- ◆ Mother, I totally and completely forgive you now.

- ◆ Mommy, I totally and completely forgive you now.

- ◆ Mom, I totally and completely forgive you now.

- ◆ Mama, I totally and completely forgive you now.

Let's call this forgiveness affirmation your **Forgiveness Goal**. It states your intention to the Universe, which is to totally and completely forgive.

Write, type or say aloud your Forgiveness Goal 10 – 20 times. Repetition is one key to success with goals and affirmations.

Now let's move on to "**Forgiving Dad**" examples:

- ◆ Father, I forgive you for not being physically or emotionally available to me.

- ◆ Daddy, I forgive you for not expressing your feelings.

- ◆ Dad, I forgive you for not telling me you love me.

- ◆ Papa, I forgive you for not touching, hugging or kissing me.

Once again do this forgiveness process on each grievance listed. Remember to take a deep breath at the end of each sentence. If you find writing or speaking a certain affirmation is too painful, do the suggestions above. **"I am willing to consider..."** or **"I'm willing to..."**

When you have completed writing numerous forgiveness affirmations per grievance, then write:

I TOTALLLY AND COMPLETELY FORGIVE YOU NOW.

- ◆ Father, I totally and completely forgive you now.
- ◆ Dad, I totally and completely forgive you now.
- ◆ Daddy, I totally and completely forgive you now.
- ◆ Papa, I totally and completely forgive you now.

Write or say this affirmation 10 to 20 times.

ONE-TO-ONE VERBAL PROCESS – EXERCISE

Another method of forgiving is to get a partner (preferably one that is open to and understands these types of processes) and say the forgiveness affirmations out loud to that person.

DO NOT under any circumstances engage in these forgiveness processes with the person you are attempting to forgive. There is no safe space created when you do this. The person has a tendency to become defensive rather than helpful.

Use your partner as a "substitute" for the person you are forgiving. Your partner should support you in every way possible. He or she should make sure you look in their eyes while saying the forgiveness affirmation. Your partner should not allow you to move from one grievance to the next before you are complete. If it is a heavy grievance, the person may have to repeat the affirmation numerous times. You can tell someone is complete for the moment because the heaviness has dissipated or you feel an energetic shift. There is a different feeling when someone has truly forgiven. It may take more than one forgiveness process to feel deeply complete.

How to do this forgiveness process:

1. Sit facing your partner. who is playing the part of the person you are forgiving.

2. Look at your list of grievances and pick one.

3. Look up into your partner's eyes.

4. Say the forgiveness affirmation:

    a. "Mother, I forgive you for …."
        If this is too painful for you, then back up and say an easier forgiveness affirmation:

    b. "Mother, I am willing to consider forgiving you for…." Or:

    c. "Mother, I am willing to forgive you for…."

5. Every time you say a forgiveness affirmation, your partner responds with one of the following:

    a. "Thank you."

    b. "I want you to forgive me."
        "Great, take a breath and say it again."

If you are the supporting partner, listen for clues that indicate the forgiveness process isn't complete. For example, if your partner says:

- ◆ Mother, I forgive you for hurting me, you witch.
- ◆ Father, I forgive you for abandoning me, you jerk.

If your partner still seems angry or hurt, have them keep repeating the appropriate forgiveness affirmation until you sense an energetic or emotional release, with no derogatory remarks or feelings. Painful grievances may take awhile. Be patient. Remember, it took years to accumulate the pain and may take time to release. Or it is possible it might be released in an instant. If you forgive **ONE** person for **ONE** thing, you will experience success. Be patient with the forgiveness process and acknowledge yourself for **ANY** successes.

I encourage you to be brave in the face of any seeming setbacks or uncomfortable feelings which arise. It is common for people to cry. I always encourage people to continue crying until they reach the bottom of the hurt. There is an old saying: "If it hurt going in, it may hurt coming out." If you experience some emotional pain while forgiving, this is a natural side effect of healing.

After you have gone through your whole list, forgiving each individual grievance, say:

"Mother, I TOTALLY AND COMPLETELY FORGIVE YOU NOW."

Repeat this over and over again - maybe 10 to 20 times.

EMOTIONAL RELEASE VISUALIZATION - EXERCISE

After you have done one of the forgiveness processes above, lay down, relax and breathe, very gently connecting your inhale to your exhale. Obviously, if you are sitting down, you will have to adjust the visualization. Starting at your feet, imagine different parts of your body relaxing.

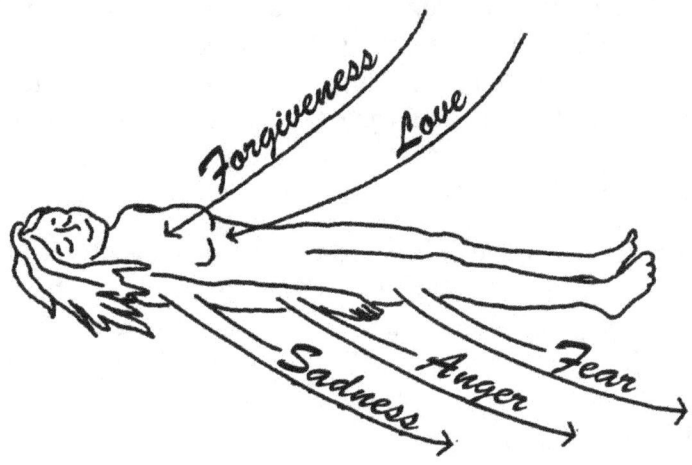

Become aware of and relax these parts of your body:

- your feet; ankles; knees.
- your thighs; your sexual area.
- your stomach; colon; semi-colon (just kidding)
- your chest; lungs; heart.
- your shoulders; arms and hands.
- your neck and jaw.
- your mouth; teeth; gums and tongue.
- your eyes; forehead; and the top of your head.
- your spinal column and then relax your whole body.

Next, search your body for any place you may have stored **SADNESS**. The way to search the body is by taking your awareness and scanning through the whole body. You may have noticed areas of tightness while you were relaxing. When you find any suppressed sadness, visualize the word "sadness" leaving your body on an arrow moving down into the ground.

When negative energy moves, it becomes neutral. Take a deep breath which will help move out the emotion.

Be sure to check your heart for any suppressed sadness. Use your breath to keep the energy moving.

After you have completely breathed out your sadness, search your body for any suppressed **ANGER** and breathe that out. See the word "anger" leaving on an arrow down into the ground.

Make sure you check your stomach and sexual area for anger - those are favorite storage spots. Then breathe the anger out. Also, notice your hands and arms for any anger stored there from the times you may have felt like hitting someone and didn't. Thinking about doing something and actually doing it are two vastly different things.

After breathing out all the anger stored within you, then search your body for any suppressed **FEAR** and breathe it out. See the word "fear" leaving your body on an arrow down into the ground.

After you have breathed out all your fear, anger and sadness, use your breath to pump out any negativity still lurking in your body by blowing it out the bottom of your feet.

You have emptied out a huge space within yourself by forgiving, breathing and releasing emotions. It is said the Universe abhors a vacuum. Now fill that space up with the word **FORGIVENESS**. Breathe it in from above. When you feel like you've taken in as much forgiveness as you can handle, take one big breath through your mouth and breathe in a little more.

Lastly see the word **LOVE** flowing into your mind and body. Allow your mind, your body and your heart to fill up with love.

This process may seem silly, but don't underestimate it. In one of my seminars a man instantly healed the top three vertebrae of his spine during this visualization.

DEAR READER,

You have just read the crux of the *Forgiveness equals Fortune* method. At this point in the reading of the *Forgiveness equals Fortune* book, I encourage you to pause. To understand, practice and integrate these forgiveness processes will help you receive maximum value from this book. If you have not yet done the exercises outlined at the beginning of this chapter entitled, "The Seminar," now would be an excellent time to do so. The power of *Forgiveness equals Fortune* lies in **doing** the forgiveness work.

People have received great value from reading this book and practicing these steps. The secret to success in forgiving is to spend sufficient time and move deeply into forgiveness. I feel certain you will discover the rewards of forgiveness will greatly enrich the quality of your life.

Below is an abbreviated version to assist you. Remember to take a deep breath after each line of writing to release the energies and emotions accompanying the lack of forgiveness. If you find yourself feeling annoyed being asked to breathe so often, you may have to add me to your list of people to forgive.

1. Make a list of the people you want to forgive: (deep breaths)

....

....

....

....

....

....

....

....

....

....

....

....

....

....

....

....

2. Choose one person to forgive by putting a star by their name.
   (Keep choosing one person to forgive until your list is complete.)

3. Make a list of the grievances you are holding against that person:
    (deep breaths after each grievance)

    ....

    ....

    ....

    ....

    ....

    ....

    ....

    ....

    ....

    ....

4. Put the name or initials beside each grievance you may hold against
    another person.

5. Write forgiveness affirmations for each grievance: (deep breaths)
    "Name, I forgive you for ... " (write in each grievance from above)

    ....

    ....

    ....

    ....

    ....

    ....

    ....

    ....

6. Write this forgiveness affirmation at least 5-10 – perhaps say it out loud as well: (deep breaths)

"Name, I totally and completely forgive you."

....

....

....

....

....

....

....

....

....

....

Notice how you feel when you write, say and breathe: "Name, I totally and completely forgive you." Do you feel more relaxed, lighter, perhaps more peaceful? Please pay close attention - so you notice the subtle benefits of forgiving.

Warmest regards and encouragement,

LIAH HOLTZMAN

RECEIVING FORTUNE - TIME AND MIRACLES

After doing these forgiveness processes, be sure to note the miracles or fortunes that may occur in your life. You might even keep a "fortune" notebook to record your miracles.

Time plays no part in the creative process of the mind. In other words, you do not have to wait any specific length of time to receive fortunes after forgiving.

You don't have to wait for miracles. Miracles are waiting for you! Many people have experienced instant miracles after engaging in the process of forgiving. One woman had a miracle show up during the seminar. She received a phone call that improved her life.

Miracles are always present. Universal Goodness is always flowing towards us, surrounding us. **Our grievances stand like a brick wall, blocking the natural flow of miracles**. When we release the grievance, the miracle may instantly appear.

THE HEALING PROCESS

In today's modern medical technology, many people rely on drugs, medication, surgery and radiation for healing symptoms.

Forgiveness is a divine healing process, which goes beyond merely healing symptoms. Forgiveness has the potential to heal the root cause of illnesses, which may be unforgiven thoughts or unreleased emotions.

BE AWARE - HEALING JUST AHEAD

When we intend to heal the source of a problem, a possibility exists that the symptoms and feelings associated with that problem may get worse before they get better. In holistic healing this is called the "Healing Crisis," a sign that true healing is taking place. As you did your forgiveness process, you may have noticed negative thoughts and unpleasant sensations passing through your mind and body.

After forgiving, you may experience some unpleasant emotions surfacing. The emotions were always there; however, you were not aware of them because they were suppressed. The good news is you are finally getting to the root of your unresolved issues. Once you release, the healing may be permanent.

Moving through unpleasant emotions or some discomfort is clearly worthwhile if you know you are healing the source of the pain or illness. Forgiveness is a good place to start in your healing process. Of course, do whatever is needed to heal yourself, which may be traditional medicine. Use your forgiveness wisdom in conjunction with anything you deem best for your health. Here's a tip: The second edition of Lauren's Alternatives for Everyone: A Guide to Non-traditional Health Care will be for sale on Amazon in 2017.

The mind can be likened to a beaker of water with mud in it. The water is the mind and the mud is the unforgiven thoughts, which are stored in the subconscious mind. The conscious mind floats on the surface. Forgiveness, or any other natural healing process, is comparable to pouring clean water into the beaker.

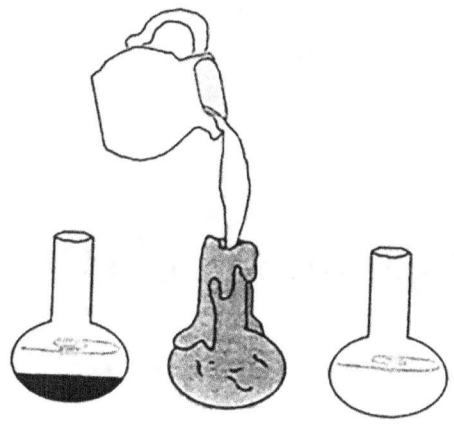

After the introduction of the clean water, the mud or subconscious thoughts are stirred up and start rising to the surface of our conscious mind. Suddenly we become aware of the muck swirling around us.

However, if we continue pouring clean water into the beaker, eventually the mud will flow up and out over the top of the beaker. We will then be left with clear water and possibly permanently healed.

Most people tend to get upset when all the muck begins to swirl around, muddying the water. They stop forgiving or pouring in the clear water and the mud settles back down. Although the water appears clearer, the mud has settled to the bottom again, clouding the subconscious mind.

Stirring up all that mud by doing forgiveness processes can be a bit tiring. You may want to stop and rest periodically. Taking time to integrate is recommended.

"Rest does not come from sleeping. It comes from waking."
- A Course in Miracles

After integrating, keep going. Your forgiveness process is working. The goal is to end up with clean water and a healed mind and body. You may want to utilize these forgiveness processes regularly, similar to taking a shower to clean off any newly-accumulated "mud."

The *Forgiveness equals Fortune* processes are a generic guideline to forgiveness success. Feel free to alter, change, improve or edit the instructions to fit your life and personality. Be creative with these tools and discover the power, effectiveness and joy of forgiveness.

Become a Forgiveness Star

CHAPTER 9
FORGIVING SELF

Grievances against ourselves block the flow of life energy - including health, relationships, and creativity. The mind or ego holds grievances. One of the mind's jobs is to protect us or so it thinks. The mind reasons: "Since I am alive now, my thoughts have kept me alive. So why change?" The mind is extremely good at protecting. But it can protect us from growing as well.

FORGIVING AND SELF-ESTEEM

Lack of forgiveness decreases self-esteem. High self-esteem cannot flourish when we have not forgiven ourselves. How can we think we are wonderful when we are carrying a load of grievances?

Some people fake high self-esteem by acting egotistical and arrogant. Often the most arrogant people feel inadequate, frightened, hurt, sad and lonely.

WHAT HAPPENED TO OUR SELF-ESTEEM?

While growing up, our parents taught us how to function as good human beings. Sometimes they tried so hard to make us good, they made us bad. At times their instructions sounded derogatory, negative and critical. We heard a lot of "don'ts" and "shouldn'ts" and "that's not right," "bad boy," "bad girl," usually without a balance of nurturing words, encouragement and compliments. Our parents didn't realize the effect unbalanced criticism would have.

We may have interpreted the critical instructions to mean we were not good enough, bad or generally a lousy human being. Their negative set of instructions wreaked havoc on our self-esteem.

As children, we may have misinterpreted our parents' words and behavior misconstruing subtle nuances of communication. I remember, as a young girl, I loved to sing. Several times I sang out in my grandest voice and my parents laughed. I interpreted their laughter to mean my singing wasn't good, so I stopped singing. I found out later they laughed because they thought I was cute. This was not criticism, although I interpreted it as negative.

Pretty much everyone, regardless of the extent of their conditioning, could use forgiveness towards their parents. Forgiving dissolves resentment, fear and sadness, which in turn raises self-esteem.

T'AINT NO ONE OUT THERE TO FORGIVE BUT ME

Forgiving other people is vital, especially if we believe we were victims. Forgiving others can clear a path to forgiving the self.

Paradoxically, other people are only a reflection or projection of our own consciousness. We are constantly creating and attracting who and what we are or were. Swiss psychologist Carl Jung has this to say:

> *"Everything that irritates us about others can lead us to an understanding of ourselves."*

Forgiving yourself comes easier when you have removed resentment, anger, fear and sadness about others. After forgiving our parents for their unconscious treatment towards us, the path is cleared for self-forgiveness. Some people feel moved to forgive themselves first. Follow your own Inner Guidance about which to do first.

FORGIVENESS EQUALS FORTUNE PROCESS RESTATED

To forgive yourself, once again follow the *Forgiveness equals Fortune* process, which was explained in depth in the previous chapter.

Make a list of all your resentments, fears and guilty feelings about yourself. Remember the negative stimulating sentences we used in the last chapter in the Creative Blame section?

I'm angry at myself for

....
Judgment

I blame myself for

....
Judgment

I hate myself for

....
Judgment

I'm afraid because

....
Judgment

I feel sad because

....
Judgment

I feel guilty because

....
Judgment

As before, say the first part of the sentence, listen to your mind for its negative response and fill in the judgment blank. You don't need to keep rewriting the first part of the sentence. Remind yourself to take a conscious breath after each judgment. You may have to do this exercise in segments because you may not have time to make a list of **all** your judgments and forgive them all in one sitting. Forgiving one or two grievances completely can be more effective than partially forgiving many.

CHAPTER 9
FORGIVING SELF

Common judgments people hold against themselves are:

- being unlikable and/or unlovable
- judging and blaming myself and others
- saying mean or cruel things
- saying or doing negative things to my children, grandchildren, step children, whomever
- not loving myself and others
- being critical and judgmental
- saying "yes" when I mean "no"
- not being a boy/girl
- not being good enough
- losing my job; going broke; failing
- being greedy; selfish; lazy
- lying; cheating; stealing
- having addictions or bad habits
- allowing people to hurt me; hurting others
- any illegal activities
- abusing myself or others

A more gentle approach can be used to create a Self-Forgiveness list by answering this question:

Something I haven't forgiven myself for is:

Then, as with the Creative Blame Process, merely listen to the responses your mind gives you and write them down.

✷

✷

✷

✷

✷

✷

✷

SELF FORGIVENESS - EXERCISE

After doing the Creative Blame process on yourself, you now have a good idea of what to forgive. To refresh your memory, you can forgive by using one of these methods:

1. Write, type or say out loud forgiveness affirmations.

2. One-to-one verbal forgiveness process with another person.

3. One-to-one verbal forgiveness process with a forgiveness coach.

Refer back to the forgiveness process in the preceding Seminar chapter to recall the details of these processes. Examples of forgiving yourself:

- ◆ I forgive myself for hurting myself and others.
- ◆ I forgive myself for not loving myself.
- ◆ I forgive myself for being afraid of people.
- ◆ I forgive myself for being greedy, selfish or lazy.
- ◆ Etc.

Always remember to do your completion forgiveness affirmation at the end. Repetition is important. What would happen if you said this affirmation on a regular basis for a week or a month?

- ◆ I totally and completely forgive myself now.
- ◆ I totally and completely forgive myself now.
- ◆ I totally and completely forgive myself now.

If you like, you can also do the Emotional Release Visualization found in the Seminar chapter. Notice as you feel lighter and filled with energy after forgiving yourself.

I'LL FORGIVE MYSELF IF I CHANGE - EXERCISE

We have a tendency to place conditions on forgiving ourselves. "I'll forgive myself if..." or "I'll forgive myself when..." If you find you are doing this to yourself, ask this question:

What would I have to do to forgive myself? Make a list of all the things you would have to change. Here are examples:

I'll forgive myself...

- when I stop being angry
- if I stop blaming other people
- when I lose weight
- if I stop being afraid
- when I become more loving
- when I become a better person
- when I become successful
- when I stop cursing - damn it!

What if you never changed? Would that mean you could never forgive yourself? Forgiveness is about accepting ourselves and other people *exactly* as we are. Are you willing to forgive yourself even if you never get any better or change? If you answer "no" to this question, then choose one of these affirmations to write so you can shift your thinking.

- I am now willing to forgive myself even if I don't change or get better.
- I am now willing to forgive myself even though I'm not successful.
- I am now willing to forgive myself even though I haven't lost weight.
- I am now willing to forgive myself because there is no reason to continue punishing myself.

After working with these kinds of affirmations, forgiving yourself should become easier.

FORGIVING OUR BODY - EXERCISE

Many people blame their bodies for their problems even though our body merely follows our conscious or unconscious instructions. Make a list of the grievances you have against your body.

✳

✳

✳

✳

✳

✳

✳

Commonly-held grievances against the body are:

- being too fat or too thin
- being sick, unhealthy or unfit
- being too tall or too short
- being ugly or not attractive
- too big or too small nose, ears, eyes, etc.
- having wrong size penis or breasts
- being the wrong sex

After seeing your grievances in black and white, the next step of course is to forgive your body.

- I forgive my body for being too fat.
- Body, I forgive you for being too tall, etc.

Then:

- Body, I totally and completely forgive you now.
- I totally and completely forgive my body now.

FORGIVENESS DIET - EXERCISE

In the Bible a disciple of Jesus asked him how many times he should forgive. Jesus replied "Seventy times seven."

The Forgiveness Diet is an idea created by Sondra Ray and developed in her book *The Only Diet There Is*. Her premise is that forgiveness releases and unblocks energy, which could support the loss of weight or other "heaviness."

The Forgiveness Diet is a simple exercise of writing or typing the following forgiveness affirmation 70 times a day for seven days:

> *I (your name) totally and completely forgive (myself or another) now*

You may want to combine the Forgiveness Diet with the *Forgiveness equals Fortune* process.

I recommend dieting on forgiveness. I cannot predict how much "weight" you will lose. All I know is you will feel lighter.

RECOVERING FROM GUILT TRIPS - EXERCISE

Here's a healing visualization to support you in handling guilt:

Take a breath, close your eyes and relax.

Now, imagine yourself coming into a courtroom as the defendant. You've had a lengthy trial where all of the evidence has been presented. The court has recessed for several hours and the judge is now re-entering the courtroom. Make the judge someone who has judged you, which could be yourself.

"All rise. Here comes the judge." The judge sits down and hits his/her gavel, demanding order in the court.

The bailiff then says, "Will the defendant please rise."

You stand up and await judgment.

The judge looks at you and says, "All the evidence has been heard. I find you innocent of all charges!"

107

UNFORGIVABLE - EXERCISE

Sometimes hidden deep within the recesses of the mind, our forgiveness work may uncover something we believe is "unforgivable." The unforgiveable sin is definitely a block to our fortune. It is imperative to alter our belief system about this so-called unforgivable sin. Ask yourself:

Is there anything I have done I think is unforgivable?

Listen to your mind and write down its responses.

✳

✳

✳

Take a deep breath and let yourself relax into this exercise. Looking at what you believe is unforgiveable is about as deep as you can get.

Some examples we may deem as "unforgiveables" might be:

- cutting off communication with loved ones
- disowning a child
- feeling like a coward
- hurting a child or animal
- lying under oath; cheating in business; stealing
- adultery; rape; incest; abortion
- criminal behavior; abuse

Use the following affirmations to dissolve and transform anything you've judged as unforgivable:

- I'm now willing to see that everything is forgivable.
- It is impossible for an innocent child of the Universe to do anything unforgivable.
- Everything I do is forgivable – no matter what.
- Life is filled with lessons – they do not have to be a life sentence.
- I forgive myself for thinking I was unforgivable.
- I totally and completely forgive myself for everything now.

Work with these affirmations until your guilt disappears and you are able to forgive yourself. Forgiving oneself completely sometimes happens in layers. You will feel complete and then another layer will surface giving you another opportunity to totally and completely forgive. So you might as well surrender and relax into the process of forgiving yourself.

CHAPTER 9
FORGIVING SELF

CHAPTER 10
ASKING OTHERS FOR FORGIVENESS

If you think someone else has not forgiven you for something you did, you may not be able to forgive yourself. One way to forgive yourself is to ask the other person to forgive you.

When someone forgives you for something you have been unable to forgive yourself for, forgiving yourself becomes easier. Another person's forgiveness opens up a huge space within yourself. One reasoning may be: "If they're willing to forgive me, why shouldn't I?"

Forgiving yourself becomes easier when you receive forgiveness from someone you have harmed. That person is your reflection. If they are forgiving you, then some part of you is forgiving yourself.

ASKING FOR FORGIVENESS FROM OTHERS - EXERCISE

Doing this process strictly internally can be just as effective as asking for forgiveness directly from another person. You have to use your intuition to determine if it is wise and safe to ask someone for their forgiveness.

- Think about a person whom you wish would forgive you.

- Take a breath, relax and bring the image of this person into your heart.

- Speak to them mentally or even out loud.

(Their name) I ask your forgiveness for anything I have said or done, either intentionally or unintentionally, that caused you pain or harmed you in any way.

Let your heart soften and open to receive their forgiveness. Imagine the person replying to you:

(Your name), I forgive you for anything you have said or done that caused me pain or harmed me. I forgive you totally and completely.

Deep breath – blowing out any residual guilt or fear.

ASKING YOUR PARENTS TO FORGIVE YOU

A great deal of emphasis is placed on forgiving our parents in this workbook. Perhaps we should consider putting the shoe on the other foot and see if it fits. Maybe it would be wise to ask our parents to forgive US.

> *What do you mean? I've never done anything that might have hurt or upset my parents! Have I?*

As children, we tend to think of ourselves as victims because we are small in size, not fluent in the language, new to the planet, and with limited knowledge of how the world works. Growing up and learning about ourselves, other people and how to succeed as a human being can be rough at times. Growing up (notice the "**ow**" in gr**ow**ing) can create emotional trauma, and forgiveness becomes needed.

Many great philosophers have compared life to a river. At times, it feels like I'm riding the River of Life in a small rubber dinghy with all my relationships in the boat with me.

While rowing down the River of Life, we pass through many different sections of the river. First, there's conception, then birth, infancy, childhood, puberty, the teen years, young adult, mature adult, elderly and beyond. Each phase is distinct from the others and brings unique challenges.

Sometimes the water flows swiftly, and there are rapids you doubt you'll get through. Other times there are rocks and sand bars, some of which are not visible. The river can be smooth and pleasant or it can be rough and frightening.

Learning to forgive the people in your boat when someone gets thrown off balance by a wave of life is mandatory. If you can't learn to work together in harmony, maneuvering your boat down life's river, then your boat might sink. The choice seems to be to **forgive** and work together or not to forgive and **sink** together. Which do you prefer?

When people are frightened or thrown off balance, they may exhibit abnormal behavior. For example, they might physically grab you or even accidentally hurt you because they fear they might fall overboard and be lost.

As children, and especially as teenagers, we were probably difficult to get along with as we paddled down the river of life. We tend to focus on the fact that our parents were difficult. Who says we weren't just as difficult?

ASKING OTHERS FOR FORGIVENESS

Asking our parents to forgive US for the unkind things we have said and done in the past could be an intelligent activity that would produce positive results for everyone. Let's start with mom.

ASKING MOM FOR FORGIVENESS - EXERCISE

Mommy, Mother, Mom, Momma, please forgive me for:

✴

✴

✴

Common grievances you might ask your mother to forgive you for:

- ◆ for being a difficult child.
- ◆ for being demanding.
- ◆ for crying and keeping you awake at night.
- ◆ for being an unhappy, angry, sick child.
- ◆ for not understanding you.
- ◆ for saying mean things to you.
- ◆ for being jealous of you.
- ◆ for being verbally abusive.

Now ask to be forgiven for more specific events that you know were traumatic for everyone concerned:

- Mommy, forgive me for screaming and throwing tantrums in the grocery store.

- Mother, please forgive me for borrowing your brand new car and totaling it.

- Mom, please forgive me for getting drunk and thrown in jail.

- Mama, please forgive me for getting my girlfriend pregnant at the senior prom and becoming a father at 17.

LET MOM FORGIVE YOU - EXERCISE

Say, write or type these forgiveness affirmations:

- My mother forgives me for being a difficult child.

- My mother forgives me for being demanding.

- Mommy forgives me for crying and keeping her awake at night.

- Mama forgives me for being an unhappy, angry, sick child.

- Etc.

Now work with the completion forgiveness affirmation 10 to 20 times as in the *Forgiveness equals Fortune* process:

- My mother totally and completely forgives me now.

- Mom totally and completely forgives me now.

- Mommy totally and completely forgives me now.

HAVE COMPASSION FOR YOUR PARENTS

I believe parenting may be one of the most difficult jobs anyone could undertake, yet it might be one of the most rewarding as well. In the past, adequate positive and effective parenting information was not available. Any training was likely influenced by the world's tendency towards negativity. "Spare the rod and spoil the child." Only recently has the concept "thought is creative" become widely recognized, helping us realize the critical importance of thinking positively, treating others with compassion, plus teaching our children to forgive through demonstrating forgiveness at home.

Even though the power of positive thinking has entered the consciousness of the planet, thinking positively requires a shift in the internal workings of the mind. Being positive isn't always easy to do. We are practicing in order to make the shift from negative to positive, which seems to be an eternal process happening in each moment.

When you think of your parents, do your best to acquire compassion for them while realizing they did the best they could - given their own negative and sometimes traumatic childhoods as well as the level of human awareness prevalent during their lifetime. Humanity is evolving into universal kindness. Karen Drucker sings a song that especially touches me, similar to the famous quote from the 14th Dalai Lama. Here is a line from the chorus: "My religion is kindness and I practice it every day."

COMPASSIONATE COMMUNICATION

If you want to practice forgiveness in your daily life, notice the way you speak to and about other people. Do your best to use compassionate words rather than unkind or judgmental words. Below is a meaningful quote from Quotes Gate on the Internet:

"The tongue has no bones, but it is strong enough to break a heart. So be careful with your words."

Shifting to a more compassionate manner of speaking can be similar to learning a new language. Many of us grew up with a very unkind form of the English language. Psychologists and sociologists have realized fairly recently that words themselves can have a formidable and often damaging impact upon people and society.

"Sticks and stones may break my bones, but words can never hurt me" is a familiar children's rhyme but is not necessarily true. Words can and often do hurt and wound. Words have the ability to injure or to heal.

As humanity evolves, a more compassionate form of English is being learned and spoken. Here are some examples of this new language:

Not Compassionate	Compassionate
Cheap	Inexpensive, reasonable, economical
Mean	Unkind, unpleasant
Harsh	Insensitive, thoughtless
Liar	Dishonest, not truthful
Cruel	Inhumane, heartless

"Kind" is the opposite of "mean." With the addition of the prefix "un" to "kind," the word is now "unkind" which is indeed more compassionate than "mean." Notice the difference in the feeling tone between these sentences:

Not Compassionate	Compassionate
You are mean.	You are unkind.
He is a liar.	He is dishonest.
She is cruel.	She is inhumane.

Using less judgmental and more compassionate language is a gentler experience for everyone, which in turn may decrease the need for forgiveness.

ON THE ROAD TO COMPASSION

If you notice you are being unkind or unforgiving, see if you can mentally move towards compassion. When thinking of the person you are having trouble forgiving, look at the challenges this person has had to overcome in their life. Perhaps this person had a very difficult or abusive childhood or struggles with a mental, emotional, financial or physical challenge. Forgiveness is an exercise in compassion. Below is a quote from *GreaterGood.Berkeley.edu* revealing scientific benefits of being compassionate:

> *"While cynics may dismiss compassion as touchy-feely or irrational, scientists have started to map the biological basis of compassion, suggesting its deep evolutionary purpose. This research has shown that when we feel compassion, our heart rate slows down, we secrete the "bonding hormone" oxytocin, and regions of the brain linked to empathy, care-giving and feelings of pleasure light up, which often results in our wanting to approach and care for other people."*

HINDSIGHT USUALLY REVEALS PERFECTION

In an earlier chapter, I talked about the "perfection" of the universe. As I edit this book for re-publication, I contemplate the last 36 years and see the perfection of my life. In 1980, right before I started forgiving my father, I experienced a great deal of emotional pain and was not making the money I wanted and needed. Now that I've forgiven him, I see my father as perfect just the way he was.

Because I wanted to forgive my Daddy, I researched forgiveness, created and led a seminar called *Forgiveness equals Fortune*, wrote this book with Lauren, had it published in Spanish, traveled to Argentina several times, and am now able to offer forgiveness seminars and coaching to those people who feel drawn to this path of forgiveness.

I am happy to have contributed to the lives of many people, as well as my own, with my forgiveness insights and experiences. I am still learning – the depth and power of forgiveness consistently dazzles me. Forgiveness feels like a Gift, representing a powerful earthly tool to lift the barriers we have installed to avoid living in Bliss (or Peace or Awe - perhaps there is no word for it). Sometimes hindsight will reveal the perfection of everyone and everything." Thanks Dad. Now let's ask our fathers to forgive us.

ASKING DAD FOR FORGIVENESS - EXERCISE

Daddy, Father, Pop, Papa, please forgive me for:

✳

✳

✳

Examples of common grievances to ask your father to forgive you for:

- for growing up or not growing up.
- for being a difficult teenager.
- for verbally abusing you.
- for blaming you for my problems.
- for not following in your footsteps in business.
- for not being as successful as you are or for being more successful than you.
- for not listening and not respecting your wisdom.
- for talking back.
- for being expelled from college.
- for getting pregnant; for getting my girlfriend pregnant
- for not giving you grandchildren.
- for showing up on your doorstep, divorced, broke and with two hungry kids.

LET DAD FORGIVE YOU - EXERCISE

Say, write, or type these affirmations:

- My father forgives me for not listening and not respecting his wisdom.

- My daddy forgives me for talking back.

- Papa forgives me for getting expelled from college.

- Pop forgives me for blaming him for my problems.

- Etc.

Once again, do the completion forgiveness affirmation 10 to 20 times as done in the *Forgiveness equals Fortune* process.

- My father totally and completely forgives me now.

- Daddy totally and completely forgives me now.

- Papa totally and completely forgives me now.

BEYOND FORGIVENESS LIES THE LAND OF PRAISE AND GRATITUDE

Sometimes it's easier for people to forgive you when they feel acknowledged by you. After we forgive our parents and hopefully they forgive us, we may find ourselves in the Land of Praise and Gratitude. It's a beautiful place filled with love, light and abundance.

When you have reached this place spiritually, write your mother and father a letter praising them for the job they did as your parents. If you survived your childhood and are alive, they did their job. Express your gratitude for how much they gave physically, mentally, emotionally, materially and spiritually.

It's okay if it takes a long time to get to this place of gratitude. Don't beat yourself up if you haven't arrived yet.

Here is a sample letter:

> *Dear Mom and Dad,*
>
> *Thank you so much for being my parents. You were the perfect people to be my mother and father. Thank you for providing me food and shelter and all the necessities of life. I am so grateful you both loved me. Thank you for giving me the foundation of honesty, integrity and stability. Thank you for exposing me to creativity, both in the world of arts and business. Thank you for the many financial gifts throughout the years of my life. I praise you both for having the courage to overcome the hardships of your childhood, the depression, the war, your own relationships, plus your children. And most of all, thank you for giving me an opportunity to be your daughter (or son).*
>
> *Love,*
>
> *(your name)*

You may have to practice writing this letter. However, go ahead and start NOW - even if it's just one sentence. Remember, what you focus on expands. If you focus on judging people and making them wrong, your judgments will expand. If you focus on praise and gratitude, what you have to praise and feel grateful for increases. If you want more positive events happening in your life, keep praising and allow the feeling of gratitude to pervade your day. If that feels difficult, go back to forgiving and most likely it will become easier. Gratitude is considered a 'gateway' habit - for it leads to other more positive habits.

ASKING FOR FORGIVENESS FROM A GROUP - EXERCISE

At times groups of people have been prejudged, harmed, persecuted, or unjustly treated by humanity. We can ask their forgiveness. Some of the groups that come to mind are:

- ◆ Native Americans
- ◆ Vietnam War veterans
- ◆ Religious or ethnic groups or races
- ◆ The elderly or sick
- ◆ Poor people, starving or homeless people
- ◆ Molested or abused children
- ◆ Mentally challenged or mentally ill
- ◆ Animals and creatures of the land and seas we've harmed
- ◆ People with physical defects

You can use the *Forgiveness equals Fortune* process by doing the Creative Blame list and then forgiving. Another method would be to write that group a letter, stating your former feelings and asking for forgiveness.

Here is a sample letter:

Dear Dolphins and Whales,

Please forgive me and the people who pollute your home and our oceans. Please forgive us for killing you slowly with pollution and quickly with our fishing nets. You deserve to live in peace – This is your home too!

Love,

(your name)

I'M SORRY, SO SORRY

In this society, we've been taught to automatically say "I'm sorry" to be courteous. Forgiveness is not an apology - you don't have to say you're sorry.

"I'm sorry" can suggest negative meanings of low self-esteem. Here are some implied meanings to avoid:

- ◆ I'm sorry. (I'm a bad person.)
- ◆ I'm sorry. (I'm pathetic.)
- ◆ I'm sorry. (I'm stupid.)
- ◆ I'm sorry. (I'm a sorry person.)

However, if you mean "I feel sorrow or sadness," then "I'm sorry" is not negative. There are instances when apologizing is an appropriate gesture, like "I'm sorry I was unkind. Please forgive me." Here are a few more examples of positive apologies:

- ◆ I'm sorry I hurt your feelings by what I said or did.
- ◆ I'm sorry we had a disagreement.
- ◆ I'm sorry I was unpleasant to you.
- ◆ I'm sorry, I didn't intend to ....

Sorrow is a legitimate feeling and is appropriate to express. Expressing sorrow or sadness helps to ease the pain or reduce misunderstandings that can arise in relationships. Caring apologies, coupled with forgiveness, can produce positive outcomes.

Some people have a difficult time apologizing because they think it makes them weak or wrong. In these instances, **you may have to accept the apology you will never receive**. On the other hand, there is nothing like a good old-fashioned apology to grease the wheels of forgiveness. It isn't absolutely necessary to say you're "sorry." You can say: "I apologize for how this situation turned out and the part I played in it. Please forgive me." Apologies can take responsibility and ask for forgiveness. Being responsible and compassionate makes us spiritually and emotionally strong.

"BEGGING" FOR FORGIVENESS IS UNNECESSARY

Begging for forgiveness is different from asking. We don't have to beg. Merely ask and then receive. Not only is begging for forgiveness unnecessary, it usually does not produce fortunate results. Most times people beg from "low self-esteem." Low self-esteem is not a natural state, but a reaction to mistreatment or a lack of forgiving the self.

ASKING GOD FOR FORGIVENESS - EXERCISE

Some believe God is all good and does not judge; therefore, God doesn't need to forgive. Remember, the only time forgiveness is necessary is when there is judgment. If you believe God has not forgiven you, you may find it helpful to ask for forgiveness. Here is one way to ask:

> *Dear God:*
>
> *Please forgive me for anything I think I may have done "wrong" or anything I have not forgiven myself for yet. I am now open to and willing to receive the forgiveness I deserve. Thank you God.*
>
> *Love,*
>
> *(put in your name)*

ASKING GOD FOR ASSISTANCE - EXERCISE

One way to make your forgiveness work more effective is to ask God, Divine Creator, Source, etc. to help you forgive yourself and others. God or Source may not need to forgive because Source does not judge; however, God is infinitely qualified to help you with your forgiving:

> *Infinite Creator – Source of All,*
>
> *Please help me forgive others and myself and be at peace with everyone. Thank you.*
>
> *Love,*
>
> *(put in your name)*

ASKING OTHERS FOR FORGIVENESS

GOD AND THE FIELD OF PURE POTENTIALITY

Some people believe that God always says "yes." This may be what Dr. Deepak Chopra refers to as the "field of pure potentiality," which can also be called "infinite creativity." All possibilities exist in the field. Anything we ask for, whether it be positive or negative, is delivered with an enthusiastic "yes." Hence, it is important to be aware of what we ask for. Sometimes being aware is not always easy because we may be asking from an unconscious place and not realize we're asking.

If this is indeed the case, then I might use this affirmation:

◆ I now cancel all unconscious, negative requests to the field of pure potentiality. Thank you and never mind!

TAKING 100% RESPONSIBILITY – HO'OPONOPONO

In an earlier chapter, we spoke about 'thought is creative' and taking responsibility for our lives. Dr. Len Hew, a psychiatrist who lived in Hawaii, was asked to work in a mental hospital for the criminally insane. This was the worst ward of the hospital, where the patients were extremely violent and the staff had difficulty staying emotionally balanced themselves.

Dr. Hew said he would work there on one condition – that he would not see patients but rather work with their files everyday, saying these two phrases: **"I'm sorry"** and **"I love you"**. Miraculously, after a time, the patients started healing and leaving the hospital. Within two years that part of the hospital closed.

In a video interview with Rita Montgomery and Dr. Rick Moss, Dr. Hew says the reason this process worked to heal the patients in the hospital was because he took 100% responsibility for his life. He asked himself the question:

> *"What is going on within me that I am experiencing people who are violent, who murder and rape?"*

He goes on to say:

> *"I am creating this experience, so I do a cleaning with Ho'oponopono by going into the Self or the Subconscious mind where the data is stored. Everything is run by information or the data stored in my mind. My experience is my stored data dancing in my life. Knowing this, I work with the data in me that experiences you as a crazy person. It is only my experience of you. If I erase that, it's not possible for you to be that way."*

This is what he means by taking 100% responsibility.

Joe Vitale, a best-selling author, world lecturer and miracles coach, discovered this wonderful doctor, learned from him and then started sharing this process called Ho'oponopono, which is an ancient Hawaiian forgiving and healing system. Joe added two more statements. Here are the updated phrases: "I'm sorry. Please forgive me. Thank you. I love you."

Nowadays, if there is conflict, upset or misunderstanding in one of my friendships or relationships, I remember to share and verbalize the practice of Ho'oponopono.

"I'm sorry. Please forgive me. Thank you. I love you."

The more I practice this clearing and forgiving technique – the more my ego relaxes and my need to be right diminishes. When I share these statements, I notice sometimes the other person relaxes and surrenders as well. I urge you to have the courage to let go of the need to be right and to forgive.

I find these declarations are very powerful and can transform an unpleasant situation into a more compassionate, loving one. What would the world be like if everyone took 100 percent responsibility for what is happening in their lives? WOW!

CHAPTER 10
ASKING OTHERS FOR FORGIVENESS

CHAPTER 11
FORGIVING OTHERS

Other people, who they are and what they do, are a reflection of our own consciousness. Consciousness duplicates itself. Our perception of others reflects back like a mirror what we think and believe, what we feel and who we are, as well as lessons we are to learn. In addition, we attract other people who possess our same faults and shortcomings, making it abundantly clear what we need to forgive in ourselves.

What we do not like or resent in others is a reflection of some aspect of what we do not like in ourselves. The reflection will be substantial enough to get our attention. Have you ever heard: "Whatever you send out comes back multiplied?"

For example, if you are consistently ten minutes late to appointments, you may attract someone who is regularly an hour late. When you realize your judgment about this person's behavior is a judgment about yourself, forgive them and then forgive yourself.

I am aware this may be a difficult concept to accept. One reason is because we only see in fragments and not the whole picture of reality. You have to become a spiritual detective to notice what is being reflected back.

A Course in Miracles has a famous quote:

> *"Love brings up anything unlike itself for the purpose of healing."*

When we are in relationship with someone we love, our intimacy makes us aware of the barriers we have to receiving love. Those barriers can be dissolved through forgiving.

Since we create our own reality, we might conclude we don't need to forgive other people, because we are the source. Don't be fooled. There is tremendous emotional value in forgiving other people.

Forgiveness erases the hurt experienced from interacting with others. If we only forgive ourselves, we miss the healing of hurt feelings and resentment. Remember, negative feelings accumulate and cause problems within the mind, body and our reality. Every unresolved relationship from the past drains off a little of our vital energy. Resolving old hurts releases energy which increases our power and zest in the present.

CHAPTER 11

FORGIVING OTHERS

PARENTS AND PARTNERS

For personal well-being, the two most important people that need YOUR forgiveness are your mother and father. If you were adopted, had step-parents and/or lived in a foster home, forgive the people who raised you, then forgive your birth parents.

Occasionally in the *Forgiveness equals Fortune* seminar someone will say, "But I've already forgiven my parents."

Usually I ask: "And when was the last time you saw them?"

I'm not surprised when they reply, "Oh, maybe five, ten, or twenty years ago."

If you believe you have forgiven your parents, spend a couple of weeks with them in their home and see if anything comes up? There is a difference between forgiving and avoiding. Avoiding is much easier to do. On the other hand, some people are naturally forgiving and don't hold grudges. You may be just such a person or you've lived long enough to have just let go. Most likely, if you are naturally forgiving, you will not be reading this book on learning how to forgive.

Possibly you may have forgiven your parents in a general way. You know - they are just human beings doing the best they can in this "crazy mixed-up world." But you may still need to do some specific forgiving of certain traumatic events.

Because the *Forgiveness equals Fortune* process is so thorough and powerful, people are surprised to discover old grievances emerge against their parents, even after spending years evaluating and assessing their relationship with them.

The basis and foundation of our whole personality is usually determined during the first seven years of life. When we're young, our mother and father are our whole world. Therefore, our relationship with mom and dad and their relationship with each other are the cornerstone of how we relate to men and women for the rest of our lives.

We relate to other people through decisions about mom and dad. Anything unresolved with our parents most likely will show up in present-day relationships.

If you decided Dad was never there for you, you might create a relation-ship with someone who, for one reason or another, isn't available physically or emotionally. This is an opportunity to forgive your father for being unavailable. As seen by this example, it becomes more apparent that: **Everyone is out to heal you**.

Colin C. Tipping states in his book *Radical Forgiveness* that:

> *"Souls collude with one another to bring about mutual healing."*

BIRTH AND FORGIVENESS

Before birth, the baby's mind is like a brand-new computer with few programs - except perhaps an operating system. At birth and thereafter, an infant makes conclusions about everything he/she experiences. Society's former lack of sensitivity to the needs of a newborn have produced negative side effects for adults. Joyfully that lack is changing and sensitivity levels are increasing.

People don't usually remember their birth, unless they do hypnosis or rebirthing. But our subconscious minds formed conclusions based on our earliest experiences, which can dramatically affect daily life. These conclusions are called "preverbal thought" because we couldn't talk yet.

Conclusions are made from our experiences with our mother, father and any hospital personnel we encountered. We may have made decisions about life based on our impressions in the delivery room. Conclusions can be made about our bodies based on what was said in regard to our size, shape, sex, weight, color of skin, hair and eyes. We also could have made conclusions about food based on how soon we were given sustenance, whether we were breast-fed, how much milk was available and if it was easily obtainable. Conclusions can be made about money from how the hospital bill is dealt with. For example, if our father felt the hospital bill was too high, we might decide we are not worthy.

These conclusions are the first programs of this life recorded in our mental computer. These programs are imbedded in our subconscious mind in the midst of discomfort, intense activity, and psychic, physical and emotional trauma. Our minds are different from computers because we have emotions. Emotions lock negative thoughts in place and influence the program or thoughts, making them more powerful.

For example, you may have concluded "Men hurt me," because the obstetrician was too rough. That thought, "Men hurt me," goes out into the Universe as a command: "Men - hurt me." After you are brought home from the hospital, an uncle walks into your room, leans over your crib and accidentally drops a burning ash from his cigar on your skin. That experience further supports your first conclusion and is added to the "men hurt me" program.

Later, when you attend school, you may have an experience of a little boy hitting you. This fits your belief system and strengthens the conclusion "men hurt me." As you grow up, other hurtful experiences with men are both produced from and strengthen the original program.

Common negative conclusions made at birth are:

- ◆ Life is hostile, painful or scary.
- ◆ People are out to get me.
- ◆ I can't get what I want.
- ◆ I don't like being here.
- ◆ I have to fight to survive.
- ◆ Nobody wants me.

Negative thoughts produce negative results. Our birth conclusions keep producing results until we "un-think" them by forgiving the people we made these conclusions about. Forgiveness erases our emotions and resentments towards the people at our birth by dissolving our negative thoughts.

Decisions and conclusions are even made while in the womb. Research is proving the fetus is sensitive to light, noise, mother's reactions, feelings, and the general attitudes and environment surrounding pregnancy. In-depth studies and discussions about womb trauma are found in the book *The Secret Life of the Unborn Child*, written by Dr. Thomas R. Verny with John Kelly. Over the years, understanding and knowledge about the prenatal experience have progressed and advanced, especially with new technology.

As you can see, there could be numerous people in your life whom you may need to forgive. Forgiving others, as well as yourself, makes room for receiving fortunes.

CHAPTER 12
HOW TO RECEIVE FORTUNE

In an earlier chapter, I defined fortune to mean possessions, money and property as well as attributes, values and inherent personal qualities. Further I stated there were two general types of fortune: *Fortunes of the Heart* and *Fortunes of the Pocketbook.*

Forgiveness is a giving and receiving process. You give up that which you don't want, such as anger, fear and sadness in order to receive that which you do want, such as love and money. The word "give" is found within the word "forgiveness."

- ◆ Give forgiveness — receive forgiveness
- ◆ Give forgiveness — receive miracles
- ◆ Give forgiveness — receive love
- ◆ Give forgiveness — receive money
- ◆ Give forgiveness — receive health
- ◆ Give forgiveness — receive peace

Forgiveness demonstrates that giving and receiving are two sides of the same coin. It goes hand in hand with the old saying, "What you give comes back to you," or "The price of giving is receiving."

After decades of research and study into human behavior, I have come to the conclusion there are just a few basic issues which prevent people from living in abundance. I believe one of those issues is the inability to receive. As we forgive, the ability to receive love, light, laughter and luxury increases.

THE THEORY OF LACK

People tend to think: There is not enough money to go around. If they receive money from someone, then the other person will be lacking. Or if they give money away, they won't have enough. These limited belief systems stand in the way of receiving. Remember, thought is creative. Strongly-held beliefs tend to become true. Therefore, if you think there is not enough money, "not enough" is what you'll most likely experience.

Lack does not refer exclusively to money. Love, health, peace, and other "fortunes of the heart" can be lacking in our lives as well.

BECOMING A SPIRITUAL FORTUNE HUNTER - EXERCISE

Make a list of all the fortunes you would like to receive. This list can include Fortunes of the Heart as well as Fortunes of the Pocketbook. Your list may be general or specific. Include some goals you are certain you will attain, as well as some goals that will be a stretch for you.

You may want to put a date next to them indicating when you would like to receive each fortune.

Sample Fortunes list – with dates if you like:

- a new love relationship
- salary increase, new job, success in business or career
- perfect new house, condo or apartment
- the ability to love thyself
- healthy body, lose or gain weight
- harmonious relationships
- unexpected money in the mail
- new car, new wardrobe, new furniture
- $.. per month or year
- trip or vacation
- inner peace and world peace
- more fun

Fortunes I Want to Receive

* ✳

* ✳

* ✳

* ✳

* ✳

* ✳

* ✳

* ✳

After making your list of fortunes, use this affirmation:

> *"This or something better now manifests for the good of all concerned and in Divine Order, for I am now consciously willing to receive all the gifts the Universe holds for me."*

The above affirmation takes care of our mind's limitations. To ensure everyone's happiness, use the phrase, "...for the good of all concerned and in Divine Order," so no one will be hurt by your fortune.

One metaphysical principle declares: We are the creator of our own Universe. Since the Universe is a field of pure potentiality, everything awaits us already.

The book *New Teachings for an Awakening Humanity* says:

> *"Yet the greatest gifts to have, and the greatest prayer to speak, is merely to accept all that has already been given..."*

If the Universe offers us everything right now, why can't we find it in our checkbook? We can liken the Universe to a wealthy father, who holds a large fortune in trust for us until we're old enough, mature enough or "whatever enough" to receive it. We must be consciously willing to receive gifts from the Universe. Gifts from the Universe may also be referred to as "Universal Bank Account," which we discuss later in the Tithing section.

FROM MILK TO MONEY - EXERCISE

Remember the negative conclusions made in the womb, at birth and during childhood? These conclusions may still be affecting our reality, even though we are not consciously aware of them. These conclusions can block our ability to receive.

Many adults were not breast-fed or were fed on a schedule rather than when they were hungry. To an infant, milk or food is abundance. If there is not enough milk or if it is not available when hungry, the baby could feel lack. This feeling of lack may later be transferred to money as an adult.

If your parents experienced poverty or feared the lack of money, you could have picked up their worries about money.

At birth if you are crying out and do not receive love, affection or food, you may conclude "I can't get what I want." This negative belief system can severely affect your relationship to money. If you want money and you think you can't get what you want, money will elude you.

If you received constant criticism during childhood, you could decide you are not worthy. This conclusion could prevent you from creating wealth. If you are experiencing unpleasant financial circumstances, look within yourself. Then ask: **"What is the source of this lack?"** You can then change the source thoughts, by forgiving and reprogramming your mind.

Be patient. Learning to find your blocks takes practice and time. Discovering the blocks does not always immediately change them.

MORE FINANCIAL SUCCESS STORIES

Let's program our minds with more *Forgiveness equals Fortune* success stories.

> The next day after the *Forgiveness equals Fortune* seminar, Max found out his new job would pay $3,500 rather than $2,600 as earlier believed.

> Laurie created $3,500 after doing two Forgiveness seminars.

Forgiveness results manifest at your current financial level. If you normally deal in hundreds of thousands of dollars, you will receive at that level of abundance.

FORTUNES OF THE HEART

Here are some more examples of Fortunes of the Heart produced by people who forgave:

> Marc found he needed less sleep and could function better.

> Sherry went home with a new, exciting lover from the Forgiveness seminar.

> Hilary had been in the process of a messy and unpleasant divorce. After forgiving, she could relate better to her ex-husband, communication improved about money and the divorce went smoother.

Georgia experienced painful menstrual cycles before the *Forgiveness equals Fortune* seminar. Afterwards, her pain disappeared.

After forgiving herself, Betsy said she felt like an old, dark energy was released. She felt renewed and uplifted – like she had a fresh start.

Lonnie forgave his son and afterwards said: "I felt like I had a sack of grain on my back. Now I don't feel like I'm carrying anything. I am so relaxed."

After forgiving his sister, Raleigh said: "I realize I have shifted my perspective in regard to my family and come to peace. Now I politely decline family invitations, not out of anger or spite, but out of a priority of choosing to be around people from whom I feel love and support. Forgiveness has completely shifted the intentions of my actions."

Cathy forgave a man who had hurt her feelings and made her angry. She knew she would be see him soon, and her plan was to give him the cold shoulder. After forgiving him, she said: "Wow, that really worked. Now I can give him a hug when I see him rather than ICE him."

FORGIVENESS IN BUSINESS - EXERCISE

I researched and practiced forgiveness because it produced practical results in my business. When business slowed down, I would type forgiveness affirmations and many times business would improve immediately. A couple of times, while typing forgiveness affirmations, I received a telephone call in the middle of the process and instantly obtained a new client.

To incorporate forgiveness into your business life and to receive more fortune, make a list of any person or persons involved in or with your business that you have grievances against. For example:

- creditors; debtors; customers; clients
- employers; employees
- banks; brokers; CEOs
- suppliers; supervisors
- CPAs; accountants; advisors
- attorneys; people suing you; people you are suing
- multi-level marketing companies and their consultants

Use the *Forgiveness equals Fortune* process on these people, groups and institutions. To refresh your memory:

1. Do the Creative Blame process by taking one of them and listing your grievances — using the negative stimulating sentences like I am angry at your for; I feel afraid about; I feel sad about; etc. taking deep breaths after each one.

2. Then do forgiveness affirmations in regard to each grievance.

3. Write, type or say the completion forgiveness affirmation: I totally and completely forgive (name).

SUING AND FORGIVENESS

Forgiving someone does not mean you have to stop suing them. Forgiveness means you release your negative or hostile energy towards a person, a group or an institution. When you forgive someone you are suing, you release the negative energy that may be harming you or blocking your prosperity. When you forgive the person you are suing, the chances of winning the lawsuit increase. After forgiving, your attitude is neutral and you are capable of communicating the situation in question without emotion, upset or bias.

DEBTORS FORGIVENESS

When you forgive a debtor, you don't have to release them from the debt. You merely liberate your pent-up fears, anxieties, anger and resentment towards the debtor. The release of suppressed emotions creates space in your mind, body and affairs. A vacuum cannot exist in the field of pure potentiality.

Since forgiveness is a positive action, the space created by forgiving may fill up with positive results. A common result after forgiving a debtor is the debt is paid off or money flows to you from another source. Here's an example:

> Stephanie forgave and unexpectedly received $189 worth of money people owed her, $100 of which she had written off as uncollectable debts.

You may forgive a debtor and forgive the debt, which means you release the person from the requirement of paying you back. This is one of the original meanings of forgiveness found in the dictionary, "...to grant remission of a debt, fine or penalty."

FORGIVING THE INTERNAL REVENUE SERVICE - EXERCISE

When I mention the IRS at my seminars, I hear groans. Many people have strong feelings, fears and hostility toward this government agency. When we are children, the authority figures are Mom and Dad and then teachers. When we grow up, we replace our parents and teachers with other authority figures. The Internal Revenue Service can become an authority figure which we believe has control over our financial lives and may stimulate fear.

Grievances commonly held against this agency are:

- taking all my hard-earned money
- making me fill out forms I don't understand
- attaching my wages
- constantly changing the rules and regulations
- being unfair; auditing me
- for scaring me and being so intimidating
- making me save thousands of receipts
- making me worry for years

What grievances are you harboring against the IRS?

✸

✸

✸

✸

Here are some sample forgiveness affirmations to write and/or say:

- I now forgive the IRS for taking all my hard-earned money.
- I now forgive the IRS for being unfair.
- I now forgive the IRS for scaring me.
- I now forgive the IRS for making me worry for years.
- I now totally and completely forgive the IRS. (repeat this numerous times)

TO WORRY OR NOT TO WORRY?

Here are a few of my favorite definitions about worry:

- Worry is interest paid in advance on something you don't want.

- Worrying is using your imagination to create what you don't want to have in your life.

- Worrying is a total waste of time. All it does is steal your joy and keeps you busy doing nothing.

- Worrying does not take away tomorrow's troubles. It takes away today's peace.

- Worry is praying for what you don't want.

Mark Twain has a clever statement about worry and yet never says the word:

> *"I have been through many horrible things in life. Some of them actually happened."*

People worry because they are afraid. Fretting and worrying does not increase income – it limits it. Since thought is creative, what we focus on expands. If we focus on our fears, odds go up we create what we fear.

> *"That which I feared the most has come upon me."* Job 3:25

Worrying, then, can be a self-fulfilling prophecy. When we worry, we focus on what we don't want, thus creating it. If we worry about being unable to pay our bills, we may create problems paying our bills.

Whenever you find yourself worrying, ask yourself these questions to help diminish the worry:

- Can I actually do something to fix this problem or is it out of my control?

- Am I worrying to avoid my emotions?

- Is this problem something I am facing right now or merely a future possibility?

If you answered yes to any of these questions: relax, take a breath and let your awareness return to the present moment. You might write or say these affirmations:

◆ I am relaxed even when I have problems to solve or issues to handle.

◆ I turn my challenges over to Infinite Source and allow solutions to appear.

◆ My mind is peaceful and focused on the present.

FORGIVENESS AND THE PRESENT MOMENT

Grievances, judgments, resentments, grudges, anxieties and hurts exist in the past, while the present moment slips away from us immediately. Here's a fun exercise I learned from Sage Hope to demonstrate the nature of the moment:

Take a breath - get ready – get set.
Okay, try to change the moment – TOO LATE.

You cannot hold onto the present moment nor change it. You can only BE in the present moment. Afterwards, you get to deal with your responses and reactions to the moment. That particular present moment has now become the past. In addition, you may also look at your concerns, desires and intentions for the future, which is a later present moment. Louise Hay says:

"When you don't flow freely with life in the present moment, it usually means you're holding onto a past moment. It can be regret, sadness, hurt, fear, guilt, blame, anger, resentment or sometimes even a desire for revenge. Each one of these states comes from a space of unforgiveness – a refusal to let go and come into the present moment."

Forgiveness is about letting go of the past and staying in the present moment or the now. "Being in the now" and "the present moment" are hot topics these days. Many of you may remember Ram Dass who in 1971 published his best-selling book, *"Be Here Now."* In 1997 Eckhardt Tolle became famous for his book, *"The Power of Now."* Mr. Tolle says:

"The power for creating a better future is contained in the present moment. You create a good future by creating a good present."

Obviously, you could create a better future when your present moment is not filled with the baggage of un-forgiveness. One way to keep the present moment clear is to accept the moment as if you had chosen it. When there is acceptance, forgiveness is not needed.

An American theologian Reinhold Niebuhr (1892 -1971) is the author of the Serenity prayer, which is a prayer of acceptance. Twelve-step programs have adopted the first verse of the prayer, and it has become quite famous:

> *"God, grant me the serenity to accept the things I cannot change. The courage to change the things I can. And the wisdom to know the difference."*

I love this joke even though it hits a little too close to home: "Today I will live in the present moment, unless the moment is unpleasant, in which case I will eat a cookie."

GIVING AND RECEIVING

The *Forgiveness equals Fortune* book is about giving and receiving – giving forgiveness and receiving good fortune. Giving and receiving could be considered two sides of the same coin. With that in mind, let's look at the way we give and our ability to receive.

CONSCIOUS AND UNCONSCIOUS GIVING

Although giving is a virtuous and enjoyable behavior, giving may not always be conscious. "Conscious" in this instance means with no hidden motives or agendas.

Examples of Unconscious Giving with Hidden Motives/Agendas:

- Giving to be liked, to buy love or to raise one's self esteem;
- Giving to be seen as a better person, more virtuous or the hero;
- Giving to avoid receiving;
- Giving because you think your gift is great (whether the receiver does or not);
- Giving because you feel unworthy to receive;
- Giving because you want to receive a positive response from another;

- Giving out of a sense of obligation, duty or compulsion;
- Giving because you believe you are supposed to give (may not want to though).

When people are unconsciously giving, sometimes they get pushy and insistent you receive their gift. They don't seem to care if you want the gift or not – it is more about them and their strong need to give.

Some people insist on being the giver. They are so busy giving there is no space for anyone to give to them. When people demand to be the only one experiencing the joy of giving, their behavior could be construed as a type of "selfishness."

Do you ever feel manipulated or uneasy when someone wants to give you something? You may be sensing or intuiting "unconscious giving."

There are a lot of givers in this world. One reason may be because much of the giving is unconscious. Another reason may be because we have been taught it is better to give than receive. In actuality, it is best to give AND receive.

Receivers are essential in order for givers to give. Since so many people like to give (whether consciously or unconsciously), receivers are needed to say yes and then graciously receive. Are you a conscious receiver?

Here is a simple step-by-step process to be a good receiver when someone offers you a gift in person.

- Take a deep breath
- Look the person directly in the eyes
- Hold out your hand and say "thank you."

That may seem easy; however, many people find it difficult to receive. Have you ever offered someone something insignificant you know they want or need and he or she says: "Oh, no, no, I can't accept that." Why not? When a person refuses a gift - is it a "conscious no" or an "unconscious no?"

When someone offers you a gift, notice how you behave. Are you aware of any thoughts, feelings, or limiting beliefs that might prevent you from saying yes and receiving? Or are you being clear in the moment and consciously choosing not to receive that particular gift? If you are consciously choosing not to receive, then a simple "No, thank you" is appropriate.

HOW TO RECEIVE FORTUNE

When children offer adults a gift like a piece of their candy or a picture they drew, saying yes is kind and opens everyone's heart. Here's a little hint about people: We're all children at heart and want our gifts received. In this instance, a sincere, conscious "Yes, thank you" will be appreciated.

Every so often I notice people give to me out of a sense of obligation because I have done something nice for them or helped them in some way. Countless people do not feel comfortable receiving. They feel they must immediately give back. Giving out of a sense of obligation is not "conscious giving."

Conscious giving is done with full awareness, being cognizant of any thoughts or beliefs surrounding the giving.

The Center for Spiritual Living – Ashbury has this to say about conscious giving:

> *"The spiritual practice of conscious giving is an invitation to deepen our connection with Spirit and to stretch our consciousness by giving with an open, joyful, loving heart..."*

Lauren, my co-author, shares this: "The more I give and receive – the more the border between the two becomes blurred. When I give, I feel as though I'm receiving. When I receive, I feel as though I'm giving."

Life flows more smoothly when giving and receiving are conscious. In order to master the principles of the *Forgiveness equals Fortune* method, one objective is to become a conscious, kind, aware giver and a gracious, deserving, open receiver. One powerful way to practice conscious giving is through tithing.

TITHING

Originally tithing had to do with crops and the land. After harvesting, farmers would return a portion of their crops to the soil. That acknowledgement and gift to the earth, through composting and fertilizing, would return to them the following year in a healthier, more bountiful crop.

Before 900 BCE the Old English noun "ti the" stood for "tenth." Traditionally a tenth of agricultural produce or personal income was set aside as an offering to God, for works of mercy, or as a tax or levy for the support of the church or priesthood. The purity of tithing may be tainted if people feel coerced to tithe. Tithing is a gift from the heart which acknowledges the abundance of life.

Tithing then evolved into an optional religious and spiritual practice. The tithing practice can be an acknowledgement to God, the Universe, or your source of strength. Some people like to tithe to their church, while others prefer to tithe to a charity or a worthwhile organization. Still another form of tithing is to give a percentage of income to someone who has inspired you, like a friend, teacher or even a stranger. Tithing gives people the experience of generosity and an opportunity to be aware of their giving practices.

When tithing, you may choose to start with a smaller percentage. Later you may increase the percentage if you desire. To stay positive about your gift, focus on the 90% you are keeping - rather than the 10% you are giving away.

When we tithe, the positive messages sent to the Universe may include:

- I have so much abundance I can give generously to others.
- I have lots of money and I want to share it.
- There is more where this came from.
- I have an unlimited supply of abundance.
- Giving money away increases my income.
- When I return money to the Universe, my financial field is fertilized and my harvest increases.

If you've never given money away for no reason whatsoever, I encourage you to experiment with tithing. You may experience a new-found freedom and joy. On the other hand, you may notice fearful thoughts come up, giving you an opportunity to clear them and focus on abundance. As you practice tithing, you may notice your abundance increasing in unexpected ways. If thought is creative and you believe you have a surplus of money, then a surplus of money may show up in your life.

Tithing does not have to be done strictly with money. Tithing can include time, gifts and services. As you experience positive results from tithing, you may want to give money. Tithing can be quite rewarding.

THE UNIVERSAL BANK ACCOUNT

This section is inspired, as well as quoted and adapted from Lauren's article entitled, "The Universal Bank Account." It is a brilliant and logical analogy of how giving and receiving works in the Universe. This article first appeared in fatemag.com and galdepress.com, April 24, © 2012 and is part of Lauren's upcoming book, Cosmic Grandma Wisdom, © 2017.

The Universe has an explicit connection between giving and receiving. The connection is like a revolving door - similar to Sir Isaac Newton's law of motion: For every action, there is an equal and opposite reaction. In other words, **for every giving of energy, there is a return of energy**.

Simply put, when a person gives, the Universe is obligated to give back - returning energy to the giver. If the Universe did not respond, it would become unbalanced. The return energy appears to come from someone else. However, the person is actually receiving back from their own Universal Bank Account. In actuality, it is the Universe giving back through whatever or whomever it has at its disposal.

One perhaps confusing aspect of this dual motion is that the energy sent back by the Universe to the original person may not show up right away. That energy however IS immediately deposited into their Universal Bank Account. In the future, when a person needs something whether it be money, a job, help fixing a tire, kindness, a hug - the Universe supplies it. The Universe then withdraws energy from your Universal Bank Account. This system of giving and receiving is moving in an infinite endless loop.

Lauren's theory is quite simple – give something each day or give many "somethings" every day. Then notice if you find yourself receiving more. You must be aware and stay alert, for it is easy not to notice the "good stuff" in life. There is a myriad of ways you can give. Here are some examples of "Gifts from the Heart" and "Gifts from the Pocketbook."

♦ ***Gifts from the Heart (To people and Mother Earth):***

- Smile at a stranger or be kind to a neighbor.
- Give someone your place in line at the check-out counter
- Be kind, gentle and generous in traffic.
- Pull weeds from a disabled person's lawn.
- Feed wild birds or animals.
- Clean up pollution or pick up trash when in nature.
- Recycle regularly and diligently.
- Volunteer to help in any way.

♦ **Gifts from the Pocketbook**

- Give money to someone who needs it: a friend, relative, neighbor, stranger or charity.

- Give money to someone who inspires you - who may or may not need the money.

- Buy groceries for someone or give food to the food bank.

- Pay the next person's toll at a toll booth.

- When someone asks for a dollar donation, give five.

- Pay for someone's education.

- Give away money for any reason that inspires you.

All the energy of your giving is deposited directly into your Universal Bank Account. Then when you have a desire or a need, something shows up to fill that need or desire. Sometimes it appears quite miraculously. The return energy is considered a withdrawal from your account. Once you understand the nature of this giving and receiving system, you may want to keep making daily deposits into your Universal Bank Account.

If you are reading this book, most likely you are a giving person. When making deposits into your Universal Bank Account, be aware that "unconscious giving" does not have the same vibrational frequency or value as "conscious giving." Conscious giving deposits more energy into your Universal Bank Account.

If we continue with the bank account analogy, conscious giving might be similar to depositing $100 while unconscious giving could be likened to depositing $10. If you are giving and giving and your life is not as abundant as you would like, you may want to determine if your giving is conscious or unconscious.

As mentioned in an earlier section, unconscious giving may have agendas. Unconscious giving could have negative patterns associated with it, like the victim-martyr pattern. A vocal demonstration of that pattern might be: "I just give and give and receive nothing in return. No one is there for me."

Another limiting agenda around giving is: "It is better to give than receive because I don't deserve to receive." Even though people are constantly giving and making deposits, their Universal Bank Account balance may increase at a slower rate than conscious giving deposits. Consciously giving from the heart, knowing you deserve all the riches the Universe wishes to bestow upon you, is a spiritually-wise way to manage your Universal Bank Account.

If your needs and desires are not being fulfilled and life is a struggle, perhaps your Universal Bank Account is **overdrawn**. The solution might be simple – start **consciously** giving and depositing energy into your Account. When things are tough, the tendency is not to give, telling yourself you don't have enough. If that's what you believe – guess what? Life will prove you correct. If you believe you always have enough to give, then your life will reflect back that belief as well. If financially strapped, start your tithing with Gifts from the Heart – almost everyone has an abundance of those.

Lauren's theory has been questioned by skeptics. What she tells them is: "Don't just take my word for it. Try it yourself - Experiment."

I too have experimented with the concept of tithing money, as well as offering my Forgiveness seminars by donation. One reason was because this allowed everyone to take the Forgiveness seminar, regardless of their financial situation. Another was to practice my own generosity.

During the contribution process, I told people: "I deserve to be paid well for my services. If you can afford to pay for yourself and someone else, please do so." With this attitude, I received anywhere from 75 cents to $240 from one person for a four-hour seminar. After seminars, people have sent me money in the mail because the seminar proved to be so valuable in their lives. If you have received value from the *Forgiveness equals Fortune* method and feel inspired to support my forgiveness work, I am open to receive your tithes and gifts. Many thanks and may your tithes return to you multiplied.

Consciously asking the Universe or other people for what you want is comparable to making a withdrawal. Once the Universe gives back, then an expression of gratitude keeps the cycle moving. This is a powerful and succinct quote by author and philanthropist, Lynne Twist:

"What you appreciate appreciates."

WIN/WIN

Money comes from other people. Businesses, banks and government agencies are run by and made up of people. It would seem the only way you receive money is from people. When everyone is happy about this exchange, it's called win/win.

Imagine what our business system would be like if everyone practiced forgiveness and took responsibility for their financial situations. The win/win attitude could become a reality. Prosperity would abound, people could enjoy their work and the fight would go out of business. It has already started to happen.

If people forgave and took responsibility, their fears of lack would dissipate. When people are not afraid, they become generous, kind and giving. I know this type of thinking is idealistic, yet I've seen it work.

Spiritually we do not win when someone else loses. Since everyone is a reflection of our consciousness and since we are all in this Universe together, if one person loses, everybody loses. This is not an easy concept to grasp.

We all live on the same planet. As communication, travel and the media become more and more sophisticated, our planet becomes smaller. Our planet is like a household, a lifeboat or a spaceship. Cooperation or the lack of cooperation can be felt by everyone in the house, lifeboat or spaceship.

WORLD PEACE BEGINS AT HOME

There are no passengers on Spaceship Earth. We are all crew members. Our job is to support our planet in healthy aliveness, peace and abundance so that the planet supports all beings living on it. A part of that job is to clear ourselves of our own negativity and grievances by forgiving and thereby supporting Spaceship Earth.

FORGIVENESS DOES EQUAL FORTUNE

The key to a successful life is to experience the greatest number of positive events and feelings over the longest period of time. More and more people are discovering the practical, tangible aspects of forgiveness improving the quality of life and increasing income. The icing on the cake of forgiveness is that it has financial and material benefits, as well as non-material benefits. By forgiving we are able to create more and more fortunes of the heart and pocketbook.

I totally support you and everyone else on this planet to live in material, personal and spiritual abundance. *Forgiveness equals Fortune!*

CHAPTER 12
HOW TO RECEIVE FORTUNE

CHAPTER 14
FORGIVENESS SUPPORT

I love sharing what I know about forgiveness and supporting other people to learn the benefits and advantages of forgiving, in order to produce miracles in their lives.

As you may have discovered from reading this book, forgiving is extremely valuable and the *Forgiveness equals Fortune* processes are simple. Forgiving, however, is not necessarily easy. Learning and remembering to be forgiving is one of the great ongoing challenges in life. Martin Luther King, Jr., said: "Forgiveness is not an occasional act – it is a constant attitude."

Even after years of employing the *Forgiveness equals Fortune* processes in my own life, I find that working with a partner is most effective for me. Working with another person creates a safe space to go deeper and sometimes provides humor to uplift the experience. Often after a forgiveness session, people feel lighter and freed from unforgiving ways of thinking and acting.

I can share subtle nuances and tools with you in the context of a coaching session or seminar that is difficult to communicate in a book. If you find yourself resistant to forgiving or feel you want to go deeper to produce faster results, please email me for further information. My email address is located at the end of this section.

ONE-ON-ONE COACHING SESSIONS

A *Forgiveness equals Fortune* coaching session in person or over the phone can assist you in experiencing more success with your forgiveness practice. Having an experienced coach support you to more deeply forgive may assist you in gently creating more space in your Life. In order for Fortunes of the Heart and Fortunes of the Pocketbook to flow to you, the space must exist in which to receive your Fortunes.

Most forgiveness sessions last approximately 60 minutes. Sessions are offered on a reasonable sliding scale. In-person sessions can be scheduled in the Phoenix-Scottsdale, Arizona, area. Please connect via email to set up **your free 15-minute phone consultation** to discuss the benefits a forgiveness session might have in your life and discover if working with me is correct for you at this time.

During a Forgiveness equals Fortune coaching session, you will learn how to efficiently use the exercises in this book. In addition, you will have assistance to resolve any issues that may stand in your way of forgiving. If some aspect of forgiveness is perplexing, I may be able to provide insight to integrate forgiveness into your specific life situation.

POTENTIALIZING SEMINARS

The purpose of the Potentializing Seminar is to raise our self-esteem through praise and acknowledgement to experience our full potential, while practicing the Language of Praise.

As children, most of us were exposed to and learned a language of judgment and criticism rather than praise and acknowledgement. Criticism has a tendency to decrease self-esteem, while praise raises self-esteem.

Since the Language of Praise may not have been spoken often during our childhood, we are unfamiliar with hearing, speaking, giving or receiving praise. Most times parents and teachers offered criticism about what needed to be improved or changed to be good enough. This had a negative effect upon our budding self-esteem.

Sections of the Potentializing Seminar

- Reframing the concept of mistakes and forgiving yourself for making them.

- Forgiving yourself increases self-esteem.

- Self-Empowerment exercise:Noticing what you like or appreciate about yourself.

- Using your intuition about others in order to give praise

- Giving and receiving praise and acknowledgement.

Potentializing Seminar Testimonials
After taking the Potentializing Seminar, Lisa said: "Receiving praise was like a warm shower of love, and I really needed that."

"I had a greater sense of self-confidence after the seminar, and I enjoyed watching other people evolve," Kathy revealed. "The seminar is both humbling and honoring, in addition to being fun."

Reverend Sherry said: "What a great seminar. I loved it! You are such a wonderful facilitator - obviously experienced, well-grounded, fully present to your participants.... and FUN. I am so glad I was able to attend. Keep up the good work.

The Potentializing seminar is wonderful for deepening the caring connection between people in existing communities, offering an opportunity to hear the positive perceptions other people have. Please contact me if you would like to hear more about or schedule a Potentializing seminar.

Liah Holtzman
Email: liah_h@hotmail.com
Forgiveness equals Fortune Facebook page
Website: http://www.LiahHoltzman.com

Happy Forgiving!

CHAPTER 14
FORGIVENESS SUPPORT

CHAPTER 15
BIBLIOGRAPHY

I thought it might be valuable to include the definition of Bibliography: "A bibliography is a list of all of the sources you have used (whether referenced or not) in the process of researching your work."

Beattie, Melody. *Codependent No More: How to Stop Controlling Others and Start Caring for Yourself*, page 144. Hazelden Foundation, Center City, Minnesota; Hazelden.org. 1986, 1992.

Bettencourt, Megan Feldman; Science of Mind, September 2016; ScienceofMind.com; Media Reviews; *"A Conversation with the Author; Triumph of the Heart: Forgiveness in an Unforgiving World."*

Chamberlain, David B., Ph.D. *Babies Remember Birth. And Other Extraordinary Scientific Discoveries about the Mind and Personality of your Newborn.* Jeremy P. Tarcher, Inc., Los Angeles, CA, 1988.

Chopra, Deepak, M.D. *Ageless Body, Timeless Mind. The Quantum Alternative to Growing Old.* Three Rivers Press, a Division of Crown Publishers, Inc., 201 E. 50th Street, New York, NY 10022, 1993.

Chopra, Deepak, M.D. *The Seven Spiritual Laws of Success.* Co-Published by Amber-Allen Publishing and New World Library, 14 Pamaron Way, Novato, CA 94949, 1994.

Choquette, Sonia; SoniaChoquette.com; On-Line Forgiveness Course.

Drucker, Karen; singer, song writer, teacher; KarenDrucker.com.

Duperon, Shawne Dr; ProjectForgive.com – A Global Resource Advancing Forgiveness Education.

Emotional Freedom Technique (EFT); *EFT Handbook* by Gary Craig. Energy Psychology Press; 2008; February 1, 2009; March 15, 2011.

Essene, Virginia (channeled by). *New Teachings for an Awakening Humanity*, The Christ. June 1, 1986, S.E.E. Publishing Co.

Foster, Jeff at www.SageHope.com

Gillis, Anne Sermons; *EZosophy: The Art of Easy or at Least Easier Living.* Easy Times Press, 52 W. Tallowberry Drive, The Woodlands, TX 77381; 2003 and 2006; Anne@annegillis.com; 713-922-0276.

Greater Good University of California at Berkley; Reports on ground breaking research into the roots of compassion, happiness and altruism; GreaterGood.Berkeley.edu

Hand, Andrew; AndrewHand.com; A Spiritual Life Center – *Neutrality and How It Can Bring Peace*; July 20, 2009.

Harder, Dr. Heather Anne. *Many Were Called, Few Were Chosen*. Light Publishing, Crown Point, IN, January 1, 1991.

Hay, Louise L. *Heal Your Body*. Hay House, Inc., Carson CA, hayhouse.com. January 1, 1978-1983, 1984-1987.

Hootman, Marcia and Patt Perkins, *How to Forgive Your Ex-Husband* seminar; *How to Forgive Your Ex-Husband*; Warner Books; Mass Market Paperback, New York, NY, October 1983.

Hope, Sage at SageHope.com

Jung, Carl; BrainyQuotes.com; cgjungpage.org.

King James Version of the Bible – Job 325.

LeBoyer, Frederick, M.D. *Birth without Violence*. Alfred Knopf, New York NY, 1975.

Len, Hew Dr., Youtube video with Rita Montgomery and Dr. Rick Moss; https://www.youtube.com/watch?v=OL972JihAmg

Leonard, Jim and Laut, Phil. *Rebirthing: The Science of Enjoying All of Your Life*. Trinity Publications, Hollywood CA, August, 1983.

Orr, Leonard. *Physical Immortality: The Science of Everlasting Life*. Inspiration University, San Francisco CA, May 3, 1981, January 1, 1982, June, 1988.

Orr, Leonard and Ray, Sondra. *Rebirthing in the New Age*. Celestial Arts, Millbrae CA, 1977, 1983.

Newton, John; Health Beyond Belief; Ancestral Clearing; at healthbeyondbelief.com; 2012-2017

Peale, Norman Vincent. *The Power of Positive Thinking*. Simon & Schuster, New York NY, 1952, May 27, 2002.

Perkins, Patt and Hootman, Marcia, Ph.D. *How to Forgive Your Ex-Husband*. New Wave Consultants, San Diego, CA. 1982.

Ponder, Catherine. *The Dynamic Laws of Healing*. DeVorss & Co., Marina del Rey CA, 1966, June 1, 1972.

Price, John Randolph. *The Planetary Commission*. Quartus Books, June 1, 1984.

Rachele, Sal; salrachele.com; Article*: Past, Parallel, Simultaneous Lifetimes*, July 2004.

Rajneesh, Bhagwan Shree and Prem Krishna. *Rajneesh Neo-Tarot*. Rajneesh Foundation International, Rajneeshpuram, OR, December, 1983. aka Osho.

Ray, Sondra and Mandel, Bob. *Birth and Relationships: How Your Birth Affects Your Relationships*. Celestial Arts, Berkeley CA, 1983, November 1, 1987.

Ray, Sondra. *Celebration of Breath, Rebirthing Book II, or How to Survive Anything and Heal Your Body*. Celestial Arts, Berkeley CA, 1983, November 1, 1995.

Ray, Sondra. *Ideal Birth*. Celestial Arts, Berkeley CA, 1985, November 1, 1995.

Ray, Sondra. *The Only Diet There Is*. Celestial Arts, Millbrae CA, 1981, November 1, 1987.

Rosenberg, Marshall, PhD; The Center for Non-Violent Communication; nvc.org; Non-Violent Communication, A Language of Life; Puddle-Dancer Press; 2240 Encinitas Blvd., D-911, Encinitas, CA. 92024.

Rumi, Jalaluddin. 13th Century Poet and Sufi Mystic.

Schucman, Helen Dr. (scribe and editor) and William Thetford (editor), *A Course in Miracles*, The Foundation for Inner Peace, P.O. Box 598, Mill Valley, CA. 94942-0598, June 1976, July 21, 2016

Shinn, Florence Scovel. *The Game of Life and How to Play It*. Simon & Schuster, New York NY, 1925, June 1, 1978, June 21, 2013.

Simon, Dr. Sidney B. and Simon, Suzanne. A Journey to Wholeness Seminar; *Forgiveness: How to Make Peace with Your Past and Get on with Your Life*. Old Mountain Road, Hadley, MA., Hatchett Books, Warner Books, New York, NY, 1990, November 2009.

Tipping, Colin C; *Radical Forgiveness, Making Room for the Miracles.* Global 13 Publications Co; Marietta, GA 30066; 1997, January 1, 2010.

Thyme, Lauren O. *Cosmic Grandma Wisdom,* Lauren O. Thyme Publishing, Santa Fe, NM, 2017

Thyme, Lauren O. *Thymely Tales,* 2nd edition, Lauren O. Thyme Publishing, Santa Fe, NM, Feb. 2016.

Tolle, Eckhardt; *The Power of Now.* Namaste Publishing 1997, New World Library, 14 Pamaron Way, Novato, CA. 94949; 1999, August 19, 2004.

Twist, Lynne at soulofmoney.org

Verny, Thomas R. Dr. with John Kelly, *The Secret Life of the Unborn Child, How you can prepare your baby for a happy, healthy life.* Dell Publishing, A Division of Bantam Doubleday Dell Publishing Group, Inc., 1540 Broadway, NY, NY 10036; Summit Books, 1981; July 15, 1982, October 1988.

Very Best Quotes; verybestquotes.com

Whittington, Michele Reverend, Creative Living Fellowship, 6530 N. 7th Street, Phoenix, AZ 85014; 602-906-4080.

Thank you for the pioneering work of the forgiveness teachers who came before me, after me and those who will teach in the future. May our combined efforts and intention assist the world to live in peace.

Warmest regards – LIAH HOLTZMAN

ABOUT THE AUTHOR LIAH HOLTZMAN

Here are some personal words and thoughts about Liah from Lauren: "One of the most delightful features of working with Liah is her consistent ability for upbeat humor.

At times, our writing process became quite challenging as we wrestled complex concepts into something simple and beneficial. We would start joking and burst into laughter. Then the situation and words magically seemed to correct themselves.

Liah is an innate and tireless explorer of all things related to forgiveness and personal, spiritual growth. Learning forgiveness through her friendship, her seminars and the writing of our book has transformed me in ways I can only describe as – awesome. Run – do not walk – to your computer or phone to arrange a session with Liah."

Liah Holtzman has had a long career of empowering others as a seminar leader, emotional awareness consultant, energy worker, breath worker, and forgiveness coach. Since 1980, she has shared the principles of *Forgiveness equals Fortune* with people in the United States and South America.

Enjoying and utilizing her love to laugh, Liah generates a humorous perspective about forgiveness, being human and increasing fortunes of the heart and pocketbook. The simplicity of Forgiveness equals Fortune principles comes from Liah's ability to make the complicated simple, through wit and brevity.

As part of her journey, she worked closely with Leonard Orr (founder of Rebirthing, a conscious breathing technique) and Sondra Ray (Loving Relationships Training), which gave her valuable insight into the power of breath and the importance of forgiveness in relationships.

In 2016, Lauren reconnected with Liah to say she wanted to prepare the *Forgiveness equals Fortune* book for on-line distribution in a second edition. This gave Liah an opportunity to edit and update the book, catapulting her into deep forgiveness research and reminding her once again of the power of forgiveness.

Liah has a spiritual certainty of the significance and importance of forgiveness in the lives of human beings and has a strong desire to support others to understand and use forgiveness principles in their quest for peace, happiness and freedom.

ABOUT THE CO-AUTHOR LAUREN O. THYME

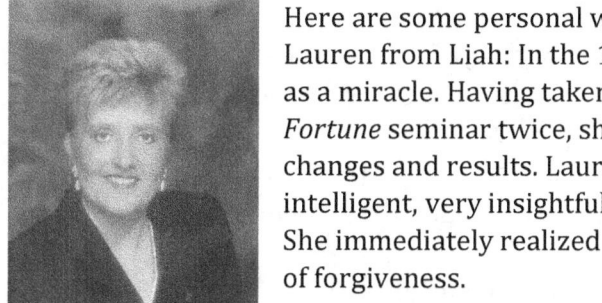

Here are some personal words and thoughts about Lauren from Liah: In the 1980's, Lauren showed up as a miracle. Having taken *the Forgiveness equals Fortune* seminar twice, she experienced impressive changes and results. Lauren is remarkably intelligent, very insightful and incredibly intuitive. She immediately realized the power and importance of forgiveness.

One of the things I love about Lauren is she is a woman of action. She was aware there was a forgiveness book inside of me and wanted to help bring it to life. Because of Lauren's spiritual insight, the *Forgiveness equals Fortune* book was born. I think of her as a Book-Wife, similar to a Mid-Wife.

Years later Lauren once again showed up as a miracle when she contacted me about preparing a 2nd edition *Forgiveness equals Fortune* book for worldwide on-line distribution, which we jointly accomplished. Working with Lauren has taught me how to write more professionally and edit my own work.

She is an excellent writer and continues to write and publish books and articles on spiritual and metaphysical subjects, as well as a practicing astrologer and psychic counselor. If you have ever wanted to write a book and just couldn't seem to get it done, you might consider connecting with Lauren and hire her as your "Book-Wife".

The following books by Lauren are available in print and ebook form on Amazon.com:

> *Thymely Tales, Transformational Fairy Tales for Adults and Children* 2nd edition
>
> *The Lemurian Way, Remembering your Essential Nature* 1st edition
>
> *Along the Nile* (historical fiction – ancient Egypt), 2nd edition
>
> *From the Depths of Thyme* (a book of poetry)
>
> *Cosmic Grandma Wisdom:* (a collection of Lauren's spiritual and metaphysical essays);
>
> *Strangers in Paradise:* (a novel of forgiveness set in Kauai, Hawaii);
>
> *Twin Souls: A Karmic Love story:* (a novel set in both ancient Egypt and modern times).

The following books by Lauren are expected to be available in print and ebook form in 2017:

> *Traveling on the River of Time*: (a trauma-free, do-it-yourself handbook for exploring past lives and healing the present); also planning stage for a CD/DVD version
>
> *Catherine, Karma, and Complex PTSD:* (non-fiction)
>
> *Alternatives for Everyone, A Guide to Non-Traditional Health Care,* 2nd edition
>
> *The Lemurian Way, Remembering your essential nature* 2nd edition

Lauren invites you to visit her websites at:

> http://thymelauren.wixsite.com/thymely-one
> http://www.LaurenOThymecreations.com
> email: thyme.lauren@gmail.com
> Facebook: https://www.facebook.com/lauren.thyme

www.ingramcontent.com/pod-product-compliance
Lightning Source LLC
Chambersburg PA
CBHW081551280526
45788CB00011B/3434